Gratitude, Grit & Giggles

Reflections from My Perfectly Imperfect Journey

Bill H.

CONTENTS

To Missy:
My Love,
My Rock,
My Caregiver,
My Partner,
My CFO,
My Life Saver,
My Catalyst for Change,
My Best Friend,
My Gratitude in Human Form.
Honey, you make me as happy as a bird with a french fry.

ACT I: THE FALL OF EGO

GAME CHANGER

THERE IS A VERY SPECIFIC KIND OF ARROGANCE THAT comes with thinking you have the world completely figured out. You build a life that looks great on paper, you surround yourself with the finest things, you pontificate on exactly how a steak should be cooked, or a cocktail should be mixed, and you convince yourself that you are the one steering the ship.

Until the day the universe decides to rip the steering wheel right out of your fucking hands.

For me, that day didn't happen in a gutter, or in the back of a police car, or in any of the stereotypical, fluorescent-lit places you'd expect a drunk to hit rock bottom. My rock bottom had a five-star view.

We were in Venice, Italy. Missy and I had just wrapped up an incredible two-week Mediterranean cruise. We were cruising in style—way out of our weight class. For two years, we had scrimped and saved, eating at home and pulling back on gifts just to afford it, completely unaware that this trip might be my last vacation—or my final experience of any kind.

And since we were taking the plunge, we did it right. We booked a suite on Regent cruise lines, complete with a butler who put our clothes away and pressed them each day. I drank mimosas every morning because they were free. We toured an Iberico ham shop with hundreds of hams hanging from the rafters, where I learned the art of "spiking"—inserting a thin bone needle into the meat so the *Maestro Jamonero* can assess its readiness strictly by the scent. We drank countless glasses of Ruinart Champagne in small cafes and museums. We bought a watch we couldn't really afford, but they were pumping us full of complimentary bubbles in the private patio gardens at Louis Vuitton—I didn't even know Louis Vuitton had gardens until I gave them some of our hard-earned money.

We were traveling with two of our closest friends, one of whom comes from a renowned Filipino family. As luck would have it, he befriended another prominent Filipino family on the ship. Soon, we were having a custom Filipino feast at a massive twelve-person table right in the center of the dining room. The second time we did it, he even got the ship's headlining comedian to join us. It was really cool to have the entire dining room staring at us, wondering who we were and what was so special about us.

We were living the absolute peak of the good life, ending the trip by staying in a luxury suite at the St. Regis. It was the kind of room that made you feel like royalty the second you walked through the heavy wooden doors, with windows that looked directly out over the Grand Canal. It was supposed to be the picture-perfect ending to a picture-perfect vacation.

But when I woke up that morning, something was fundamentally wrong.

I was a professional drinker. I knew exactly how to manage a hangover. I knew the exact ratio of water, aspirin, and sheer willpower required to get out of bed, put on a nice shirt, and pretend everything was fine. But this wasn't a hangover. My body felt toxic. It felt like an engine running completely out of oil, grinding its own gears into a fine, metallic dust. I was sweating, exhausted, and sick in a way I had never felt before.

I dragged myself out of the massive, plush bed and stumbled toward the bathroom. Before I could even turn on the marble faucet to splash some life into my face, Missy walked in.

She stopped dead in her tracks.

She didn't gasp. She didn't yell. She just stared at my face with a look of absolute, unadulterated horror.

"What the fuck is wrong with you?" she asked.

I froze, my hand hovering over the sink.

She took a slow step closer, her voice dropping to a terrified whisper. "Bill... your eyes are yellow."

I turned to the mirror. I wasn't just tired. I wasn't just bloodshot. The whites of my eyes were glowing with a sickly, unmistakable, neon-yellow hue. My skin had a weird, jaundiced tint to it. My liver—the silent, abused workhorse that had processed decades of perfectly crafted martinis, expensive wines, and relentless, unapologetic excess—had finally clocked out. It was actively shutting down while I stood there in a luxury Italian hotel.

Even then, staring at my own dying reflection, my massive ego tried to take the wheel. The delusion of the alcoholic brain is a spectacular thing to witness.

It's fine, my brain immediately told me. *You just pushed it a little too hard on the cruise. It's the rich food. It's exhaustion. We'll get some water, we'll get on the flight, and we'll handle it quietly when we get home. You can manage this.*

That was the ultimate lie of my disease: the absolute, unwavering delusion that I could manage the unmanageable.

"Well, that's a trip to the emergency room," I said, trying to inject some casual authority into my voice. But there was absolutely no way I was seeing a doctor outside the good old USA. So we hastily packed up our bags and headed to the airport. We left behind the warm, cozy suite with its antique embellishments and lovely European window coverings, and made a run for it.

I vaguely remember the boat ride to the airport. It should have been a miserable, terrifying trek, but my adrenaline was kicking in hard. The night before, the canals had smelled of stale water, but that morning, the air was sharp, fresh, and salty. We cut through the smooth water, bouncing slightly over the occasional wake from passing boats, the sweet morning breeze hitting my face. For a brief, delusional moment, I felt like I was in a James Bond movie, racing down the Venetian canals on some high-stakes mission. If I hadn't been actively dying and on my way to a hospital, it would have been a perfect cinematic ending to the trip.

While we rode, my mind started racing backward. The night before, my wife had noticed something was off with me. I couldn't remember much of the evening, except for drinking a truly crappy dessert wine. Suddenly, a new panic hit me. I was pissed. *Was that my last drink? That garbage?* But Missy, God bless her, reminded me that I'd also had a gin on the rocks in bed after that.

Instant relief. My final drink was actually something I liked: Ahh, the beautifully deranged mind of an alcoholic. My liver was shutting down, my eyes were glowing yellow, I was fleeing a foreign country for emergency medical care, and my primary source of comfort was knowing my final drink was a proper gin. Our brains just don't work like "normies."

The flight home was a blur. We were in business class—glorious, with enough room to stretch out and sleep. My feet were so swollen with retained fluid that they barely fit under the seat in front of me, but I managed to doze off.

And oddly enough, for a guy who always had a drink in his hand, I didn't touch a drop on that plane. They offered me free booze, the good stuff, and I said no. Deep down, past the ego and the denial, I knew another drink could be the one that finally killed me. That "no" at 30,000 feet was step one into an entirely new world.

We finally landed in the greatest country the world has ever known. After greeting our beagles, Joy and Lilo, we headed straight to the emergency room.

The stark reality of that hospital bed loomed in front of me. The truth finally pierced through the thick fog of my ego. I was out of answers. The party was over. The bill had finally come due, and my pockets were completely empty.

This isn't a story about a guy who just needed to slow down and drink a little less. This is the story of a guy who had to completely burn his old life to the ground so he could figure out how to survive the new one.

If you think the lighting in an airplane cabin at midnight is bad, it is practically warm and inviting compared to the harsh, sterile glare of an emergency room. We walked through those sliding doors, and the atmosphere immediately shifted. It was dead quiet, save for the random, hollow sounds of a children's program flickering on a TV in the waiting room.

Within hours, I was officially admitted. I ended up spending four or five days in that hospital. I was lucky enough to get a private room. It even had a nice-sized window seat that was just short of being comfortable enough for a nap. Looking out that window, I had a lovely view of the dry Southern California hills, speckled with hints of orange, red, and green. On clear days, I could actually see the trails and watch people hiking, just enjoying the outdoors. I remember staring out at them, trapped in my bed, quietly wondering if I would ever be able to do something as simple as that again.

It is incredibly easy not to drink when you are hospitalized. But everything else? Everything else is hard. Going to the bathroom becomes an ordeal, you get stuck with countless needles for endless blood tests, and trying to sleep through the relentless symphony of machine beeps is impossible.

And then there is the food. Hospital food tends to be below

average even when you're healthy, but when you have a failing liver, salt becomes your mortal enemy. Imagine bland, gray, pre-cooked hospital food served with absolutely zero salt. It was literally like eating grey, on grey, on beige. Even the trays it was served on were that specific shade of green only seen in hospital cafeterias. Maybe puke-green is just the cheapest color available. Honestly, I would have starved to death right there in the bed if it hadn't been for the chocolate pudding, which was the only food I could actually stomach.

But the bad food and the needles were nothing compared to the doctors.

One life lesson I already knew, but tended to forget when my ego took over, was violently reinforced during that stay. One of the first doctors I met came into my room, stood over me, and proceeded to scold me like a child for my drinking. He all but told me I was going to die right there in that bed because of my careless behavior. He looked down at me and actually said, "I could release you so you can get your affairs in order".

Let me tell you, it really sucks to lie in a cold, bland, beige, sterile hospital room, hooked up to constant machine beeps with tubes sticking out of both arms, watching people with walkers and humans in beds being pushed past your door, and be told exactly how it is going to end for you. For the first time, I realized it really could end for me that way.

Thankfully, that wasn't the only doctor I saw. The first time I met with my primary doctor, the entire dynamic shifted. She gave me hope. She sat down, looked me in the eye, told me recovery was possible, and laid out a clear, actionable path to living a longer life. What a massive difference from the first guy, who made it sound like they should be measuring me for a coffin! It was a stark reminder of an old truth: you catch a lot more flies with honey than you do with vinegar.

But the honey didn't change the severity of the diagnosis. When the official news finally came down, I felt like all the air had been violently sucked out of the room.

My liver had failed. I had cirrhosis. The only way forward—my only chance at survival—was a full liver transplant.

And there was a massive catch. To even qualify to get on the waiting list for a new liver, I had to be completely sober for six months. And by "sober," they didn't mean "not drunk". They meant absolutely zero alcohol—not even a sip of NyQuil. No more drinking. Ever.

This was devastating news for multiple reasons. First, I genuinely liked drinking. Second, so did most of my friends. Third, my entire professional career revolved around selling alcohol. My identity, my social circle, and my paycheck were all drowning in booze.

But sitting there in that bed, none of that mattered. It wasn't even a tough choice. I made the decision right then and there: no more drinking, and no more career.

Why? Because I will never, ever forget the look of absolute horror on my wife's face at the Venice airport. We had just finished a once-in-a-lifetime vacation, and instead of glowing with memories, she was devastated, terrified that I was going to die right in front of her. I couldn't let that happen. I wasn't going to put her through that kind of pain again.

She didn't know it at the time, but in that exact moment, her love saved my life. I used to roll my eyes at the whole "soulmate" concept, but now? If you find yours, you hold on to them with everything you've got. Missy is my rock. She carries herself with such incredible dignity and strength. She laughs and cries just like everyone else, but her humor is completely unique, and her love is unwavering. She is a real-life superhero.

I had made the choice. But making the choice and doing the actual work are two very different things. The doctors had a plan for my recovery, and it involved group sessions for people with failing livers and mandatory attendance at Alcoholics Anonymous meetings.

Wait, what?

Me? A drunk? Are you fucking nuts?

Just Because It's in a Martini Glass...

Let's pause the hospital monitors for a second.

You might be wondering how a guy goes from facing a literal death sentence in a sterile, beige room to what you are about to read in this chapter. The answer is simple. It is the absolute core of the alcoholic disease:

Ego.

Before I finally surrendered, I was the ultimate pontificator. Think of a Tim Allen character—the guy standing in the back-yard holding a pair of tongs, passionately lecturing the entire neighborhood on the exact right way to calibrate a lawnmower engine or sear a ribeye... completely oblivious to the fact that his own house is on fire.

That was me.

So for the next few chapters, understand this: you're not hearing from the man I am today. You're hearing from the drunk.

This is me playing me.

This is what it sounded like inside my head while my life was falling apart—and I had no idea.

I'm going to go on. And on. And on.

Because that's what I did.

And now you're the poor SOB who sat down next to me at the bar.

So buckle up.

I'm about to explain how I had everything figured out... while I was burning the whole thing to the ground.

I had an expert opinion on absolutely everything. My brain was a relentless, obsessive machine that demanded to be right. I firmly believed that if I knew the microscopic details, the history, and the absolute "correct" way to do things, then I was in control.

And if I were in control, then I couldn't possibly be a drunk.

If you want to understand how a high-functioning alcoholic

brain justifies drinking itself to death, you have to understand this obsessive need to romanticize and control the details.

Just because someone calls it something doesn't make it so.

Bear with me for a moment.

The Walking Dead is not a zombie series.

It looks like one. It's marketed like one. Hell, it's filled with zombies. But that's not what it's about. It's about people—how they behave when everything falls apart. The zombies are just the backdrop.

My drinking worked the same way.

It looked like sophistication. It looked like taste. It looked like a guy who knew exactly what he was doing.

But that's not what it was.

Another classic example of things not being what they are called is *Star Wars*. It is a Western, not a sci-fi movie. It just happens to take place in outer space.

The world is full of things that aren't what people claim they are. A jellyfish is not a fish. It has no gills. A koala bear is not a bear. Peanuts and coconuts are not nuts. White chocolate isn't chocolate.

And a martini?

Well... apparently nobody on earth knew what that was except me.

With all that behind us, I'll get to the point of this reflection: Martinis.

Because my relationship with alcohol worked the exact same way as those TV shows and historical facts.

It looked like one thing. But it was actually another.

It looked like sophistication. But it was actually poison.

A martini that is made in the United States of America with anything other than gin and vermouth is NOT A MARTINI!

End of discussion.

No other comments should need to be made.

But of course… I had more comments.

A lot more.

Because this is what my brain did, it didn't just accept things —it defined them. It categorized them. It corrected them. If there was a right way to do something, I was going to find it, memorize it, and make sure everyone around me knew it too.

The Origins

The origin of the martini is a subject for debate. Some believe it was named for the great vermouth house of Martini and Rossi. To me, that does not make sense because when you order a martini in Italy, you get a glass of vermouth. That is why they ask you if you want a sweet or dry martini. What we call a martini, they call an American Cocktail.

So the classic martini is gin and vermouth. That is like saying the classic tire is made of rubber or the classic chocolate chip cookie has chocolate chips in it. No shit, Sherlock. It is two spirits: first gin, then, in less quantity, vermouth, chilled with ice, and that is it.

Unless, of course, you start paying attention… which I did.

We can debate whether it came from the Martinez Cocktail in Martinez, California. Harry Johnson had a version in 1888. Jerry Thomas mentioned it in 1887. Boothby had it in 1907. Some say New York in 1911.

I knew all of this.

Not casually—specifically.

Dates. Names. Arguments. Corrections.

I didn't just drink martinis.

I defended them.

And looking back, that should have been a clue.

Because normal people don't need this much information to enjoy a drink.

Whenever and wherever it was created, it was gin and vermouth.

Why did they dilute the gin with ice by shaking or stirring it? Prohibition. The gin sucked because it was all illegal and made literally in bathtubs, so you had to cut it with the ice or destroy your throat. You could serve it on ice in the '20s, but the water supply was often worse than the badly made gin.

We were literally masking poison with freezing temperatures.

A tradition I proudly carried into the 21st century.

Bond, James Bond

This drink has helped many of us alcoholics find our drinking ways through glamorization. We all know James Bond's "shaken, not stirred." But James was not actually the first to say that on film. Dr. Julius No said it first—and he ordered vodka, not gin, which should have been a clue he was the bad guy.

Fun fact: James didn't say "shaken, not stirred" until the third Bond film. In *Casino Royale*, he orders a Vesper—half gin, half vodka, with Lillet instead of vermouth.

Also, *I Dream of Jeannie* had a martini fountain. Hawkeye Pierce made gin in his tent on *MASH*. *Mad Men* drank more martinis than water. Dean Martin… well, there is Dean Martin and booze.

Historic Martini Drinkers: Winston Churchill, Humphrey Bogart, James Bond, Marilyn Monroe, Frank Sinatra, Audrey Hepburn, Cary Grant, Sophia Loren.

Me.

Well, I am not a celebrity, but I can sure as shit drink like one.

That was the point, wasn't it?

If I could line myself up with that list—if I could put myself somewhere between Churchill and Sinatra—then what I was doing didn't feel like a problem.

It felt like a lifestyle.

What About Vermouth?

While we purists are in the minority, truth is on our side. I guess I can give you gin and vermouth on the rocks as a martini, but it really isn't—it's a cocktail.

Vermouth has fallen out of favor today. Mostly, I think because the vermouth Europe exports to us is shitty compared to what they keep at home. There are some very good vermouths made in the U.S. now. Quady's VYA, both sweet and dry, are excellent.

Andy Quady used to joke that VYA stood for "Vermouth, You Asshole."

Of course he did.

And of course I loved that.

Because I had opinions about all of it.

Strong ones. Precise ones. Unnecessary ones.

I knew what was good. I knew what was garbage. I knew what belonged in a proper martini and what didn't.

Or at least, I thought I did.

Because if I could get this right—if I could define it, refine it, correct it—then maybe I wasn't just a guy drinking himself into liver failure.

Maybe I was a guy who knew exactly what he was doing.

Nothing like a Good Bartender

Funny story about a skilled bartender.

I would drink Beefeater or Bombay Sapphire at home because both made good martinis and mixed well if I wanted a gin and tonic. But when I went out—which was basically every day I wasn't at home—I'd ask for Boodles. My second favorite gin. (The Botanist is actually my favorite, but I had a system.)

Of course, I had a system.

I used to frequent the Parkway Grill in Pasadena, a lovely restaurant with an even better bar. When I was working near the

San Fernando Valley, I was there so often it became my office away from the office. When you work the streets as a salesman, you learn the important things—best bathrooms, easiest parking, strongest drinks.

Before cell phones, I also knew exactly where to find the best payphones.

For more than ten years, I found myself at Parkway about once a week. I'd sit at the bar and wait for a table, which really meant I'd order a drink.

I never asked the bartender his name.

I didn't need to.

The second I walked through the door, he'd start making my Boodles martini—shaken, ice cold, served up with olives.

No conversation. No questions. Just execution.

Through a series of job changes, I stopped going there for about five years. When I finally walked back in to meet a friend for lunch, I went to the men's room first.

When I came out, there on the mahogany bar...

was my drink.

Boodles martini. Extra chilled. Olives. Waiting for me.

That day, I saw three old friends—my bartender, my lunch companion...

...and my martini.

And at the time, I didn't think that was a problem.

Gin or Vodka?

Whenever I hear someone order a martini and the bartender asks, "Gin or vodka?" I want to jump in and say, "Would you ask if someone wanted apples or oranges in their apple pie?"

They are different things.

What we call a vodka martini is actually a Kangaroo Cocktail. Originally called a Kangaroo Kicker in 1943, it was later shortened to Kangaroo Cocktail. Before that, it was just vodka up.

But sure—let's call everything a martini.

That seemed reasonable to me.

Proper Martinis

Now that I have cleared up what a martini actually is, let's talk about how it should be served.

The real recipe is two parts gin, one part dry vermouth, shaken or stirred, strained into a martini glass, and served up.

And yes—shaken or stirred.

Despite everything I just said, I didn't actually have a strong opinion on that. At home, I shook them because it was easier. If I bought a high-end gin, I'd take the time to stir it.

Either way, you want a little dilution, a serious chill, and those tiny ice shards floating on top.

That's the detail that mattered to me.

That's what I focused on.

Because most vermouth sucks, martinis today are often

ordered dry (less vermouth) or extra dry (barely any). Sometimes, bartenders will pour vermouth into the glass, swirl it around, and dump it out when someone orders extra dry.

Bone dry—no vermouth at all—is exactly that:

a glass of chilled, diluted gin.

This is how I ordered mine:

"Extra dry martini, please." "Any vermouth?" "Nope. Just a big glass of chilled gin."

Technically not a martini. Since there's no vermouth.

After all, a chocolate chip cookie without chocolate chips is just a sugar cookie.

I wasn't ordering a cocktail.

I was ordering a glass of straight, unadulterated poison…

and demanding they serve it to me perfectly.

Martini garnishes are simple: olives or a twist.

And when I say olives, I mean green olives with pimentos. Blue cheese is a salad dressing ingredient, and jalapeños belong in Mexican food. Keep them out of my damn gin.

That's it. All she wrote.

Anything else is not a martini.

There is one variation I'll concede: dirty.

That's olive brine.

You can order dirty, extra dirty, or filthy, depending on how much liquid you want floating in your drink.

Personally, I think it's for people who don't actually like the taste of alcohol.

But again… I had opinions.

The Fake Martinis

A Gibson is a martini with a cocktail onion instead of an olive or twist. One small change, and it becomes a different drink.

And yet we call anything poured into a martini glass a martini.

We would never pour something into a rocks glass and call it an Old Fashioned if it wasn't one.

So why do we do it here?

Marketing.

The dark art of making things sound classier than they are.

When you go to a restaurant, they have a wine list, a spirits list, and now—a martini list.

That should just be a list of gins.

Everything else is a cocktail.

But calling it a martini makes it sound elegant.

To me, it just sounded wrong.

Some popular "martinis"... not:

- **French Martini** — fruit juice and vodka
- **Lemon Drop** — sweetened lemon juice and vodka
- **Appletini** — awful. Just awful.
- **Cosmopolitan** — basically adult soda
- **Espresso Martini** — depends where you are, could be great or syrupy garbage

Just about every fruit juice imaginable has been mixed with

vodka, poured into a martini glass, and given a sophisticated name.

And I had an opinion about every single one of them.

Of course I did.

Because if I could explain it well enough… If I could define it precisely enough… If I could be right about it…

Then I didn't have to look at the one thing I was completely wrong about.

Who else, other than an alcoholic, would spend this much time explaining why his murder weapon of choice is so special?

INTERLUDE: I Am Bill.

Let's get off the barstools for a second.

I know the guy in the last chapter was an asshole. I know him intimately, because he was me. And if you're wondering why you should keep reading a book written by a guy who demanded his gin be served with mathematical precision while his life burned down, I don't blame you.

So let me give you a glimpse of who I am now.

I promise this isn't a conversion trick. It is just a rigorously honest reflection on how I finally learned to keep my side of the street clean, bury my massive ego, and reunite with my truth.

After decades of anger, distance, and self-guided spirituality, I've started going back to Mass. Not just on holidays. I go on Tuesdays and Thursdays. I have been going for a year now, and it's sticking.

Why does that matter?

Because I finally care again, and I believe God does, too.

For a long time, I rejected being Catholic. I was hurt and angry at the Church. I was embarrassed by its scandals. If anyone asked, I'd say, "I was raised Catholic," but I didn't claim to be one anymore. I'd say something like, "I believe in God, but it's between Him and me."

Since I was very young, I've believed in God. It just made sense to my young brain. As I grew up, that belief in a higher power and a creator only deepened. It helped that much of my social life was tied to the church and, by extension, faith. I was in our church choir at age eight. I couldn't sing well, but I was loud. I made great friends there. Fifty-five years later, my closest friends are still some of the kids I sang with—and the grown-ups who watched over us in that choir.

Faith continued to grow in me. It always made sense that there was a creator. I couldn't believe this planet, with its creatures, ecosystems, and delicate balance of life, was all by chance. When scientists claimed there was no proof of God, it sounded to me like they were promoting their own far-fetched ideas. That there's no ultimate design? That seems silly—sorry, atheists. I love you and respect you, and I hope you respect my beliefs, too. But for me, logic supports a creator.

Here's just one example: the A.A. Big Book. I find it hard to believe that two drunks wrote a book over eighty years ago that would go on to save millions of lives—and that divine intervention wasn't somehow involved.

So what happened?

Well, if you don't know what rocked the Catholic Church in

the early 2000s, you'll have to Google it. I'm not giving that evil any space here.

Two things brought me back to my roots.

First, my best friend—yes, one of the choir kids—who never strayed from his faith, gave me a book. He and his wife live their beliefs "in all their affairs," a phrase we use in A.A. to describe walking your spiritual talk in every part of your life, not just when it's convenient. The book was *A Letter to a Suffering Church: A Bishop Speaks on the Sexual Abuse Crisis*. In it, the author encourages Catholics not to walk away, but to stay and fight for the Church against the evil that had overtaken good men. The book didn't completely change my mind, but it opened a door. And not just any door—more like those floor-to-ceiling glass walls in fancy Hawaiian homes, the ones that tuck away completely so the whole room becomes open air. It was that kind of opening. Spacious. Unexpected. Transformative.

With my anger softened, I became "Catholic Light"—not to be confused with a "Cafeteria Catholic." I wasn't picking and choosing doctrine; I just wasn't paying attention to anything the Church had to say. I had faith, but not religion. I was spiritual, my way, with no structure or direction. I believed in God, but strictly on my own terms.

To be honest, I looked at my Catholic friends and envied their faith. I envied the guidance and grounding their religion gave them. But I told myself I was too smart (read: self-centered), too busy (read: full of excuses), too sure I had a direct line to God (read: ego), and too strong to need a church community (read: lack of humility).

Then God sent me a call I couldn't hang up on. My liver stopped working because I drank too much.

That's a story I will tell you in a few chapters. For now, let's stick with the part where I found my way back to the Church.

I'm proud that even as I lay in that hospital bed, I trusted that God had a plan. I didn't know what it was, but I was okay with whatever happened. I was ready to die. But then something shifted: I couldn't leave my wife alone. I told God that if it were up to me, I wanted to live. But I'd accept His will, either way. And I meant it. I didn't beg for my life—I prayed for my wife's happiness.

Funny enough, the thing that brought me all the way back to Catholicism wasn't officially religious at all—it was Alcoholics Anonymous.

A.A. insists it's not a religious organization, and that's true. You don't need to believe in any specific version of God. Your "higher power" can be anything greater than you. That openness is what made it possible for me to reconnect with my faith in the first place. Ironically, the most nontraditional spiritual tool I've ever used has done more for my Catholicism than anything since my mom.

I began working the Twelve Steps. The first three can be summed up by a simple prayer I heard somewhere along the way:

"I can't. He can. So I'll let Him."

That's really all we Catholics need to know, isn't it?

When I was a kid, I heard a priest say, *"All for the love of you, my God."* I started saying it too, probably ten times a day for forty years. But now? I realize it was mostly lip service. God knew the truth even when I didn't. *All* for the love of God? That's more of a Mother Teresa thing. That's not me. Not yet, anyway.

But I'll tell you what I can do: I can live by *"Thy will be done."* That one, I can get behind.

The Big Book says, *"We are not saints. The point is that we are willing to grow along spiritual lines."*

That I can do.

As I moved forward in recovery, I saw how central forgiveness is to sobriety. Holding onto resentment is just renting your sobriety—you won't own it until you let that stuff go.

How do I let go? I do what A.A. and the Church both suggest: I pray for the people who've hurt me. I look for my part in the pain. There's always something. Even if it's just holding onto anger or failing to pray for someone, I have a part.

And slowly, as I started living more like a sober man, I started living more like a Catholic again. I prayed more. I listened more. I walked into a church one day, not angry at the priest on the altar for the actions of others. I listened to the Word. I was moved. I felt something I hadn't in years—faith, without the filter of resentment.

I told my very Catholic friend about this, and he was nothing but supportive, just like he had been when I was lost. He always knew I'd find my way back, and he was right. Now, I go to church twice a week. If I can get to five A.A. meetings a week, I can get to Mass on Tuesdays and Thursdays.

There's a reason I go on weekdays, but that's another story. It's not about avoiding scandal or old anger—I've put those resentments to rest. Those responsible will meet their Maker. It's not my job to judge. It's my job to pray for them, and for God to restore them to who He meant them to be before evil got in the way.

I love Mass now. My parish has a school, so the kids are there during weekday Masses. It's a joy to hear them sing. Every Tuesday, we sing *Immaculate Mary* as the recessional hymn. And look at that—I'm a "we" again at church. I didn't think I'd ever say that.

Immaculate Mary has always had special meaning for me because my mom loved the Blessed Virgin deeply. The first time I heard that song again, I saw those kids turn toward the statue of Mary, and I felt the peace in that sanctuary. Tears came to my eyes. I knew I was in the right place. I felt my mom's hand on my shoulder, from heaven. It took a while, but Mom, I made it back.

I've come full circle.

I even went to confession. For a long time, the idea of a man delivering my penance kept me away. In A.A., the Fourth Step is a moral inventory, and the Fifth Step is sharing it with God and another human being—usually a sponsor. They don't hand out ten Hail Marys and fifteen Our Fathers, but they do tell you to read the Big Book. It's not penance, exactly, but it sure feels like it sometimes.

When I finally went back to confession, I realized something profound. Like a Fifth Step, when you finish it—if you've been truly honest—you feel free. It was grand.

I've loved the Church. I've hated it. I've flirted with it. I've made excuses. But the truth is, the Church doesn't demand anything from me that I can't give. If I perceive flaws in it, that's my opportunity to reflect on my part in that disappointment.

At its heart, the Church is about Jesus Christ. And my job is to stay devoted to Him. If anything gets in the way of that, it's on me—and I owe God an amends.

I've made those amends. To God. To His Son. To the Holy Spirit. And every day, I rejoice that I am one of God's kids, playing in the sandbox with the rest of His children.

At A.A. meetings, you start by identifying yourself.

Hi, I'm Bill, and I'm an alcoholic.

At first, that was easy—it was just something I said. Then it got harder because I realized it was true. Now? I say it with much gratitude. I have a disease. I take my medicine. And I'm winning against something relentless.

My Catholicism was a lot like my alcoholism. I hid it. I pretended it didn't exist. I was embarrassed to belong to a church that had witnessed such ugliness. I was ashamed of how the Church treated gay people. You can even look through history and find wars and murders done in its name.

But in the end, all that is the weakness of men. It has nothing to do with the glory of God.

Now I know who I am.

I am Bill. And I am a Catholic.

Music According
to Bill

If you thought my obsession with a glass of chilled gin was exhausting, buckle up.

Because when it came to music, my ego didn't just take the wheel—it owned the entire fucking highway.

In my mind, there were two types of people in the world:

People who understood real music…

and people who were completely full of shit.

I didn't just listen to music.

I curated it.

I judged it.

I weaponized it.

If I walked into a bar or restaurant and heard manufactured, auto-tuned pop garbage over the speakers, I didn't just dislike it —I judged the character, intelligence, and moral fiber of the person who owned the place.

Because clearly, if you didn't agree with me…

You were wrong.

* * *

Just like my rigid, unbreakable rules about what constituted a real martini, I had absolute, non-negotiable laws about what constituted real music.

You have to remember, every professional drinker needs a soundtrack.

You don't just sit in silence and drink yourself to death.

You build a vibe.

You create an atmosphere that makes what you're doing feel intentional… even meaningful.

If I were holding court at the Parkway Grill, or sitting at home with a shaker full of Boodles, I needed the right music playing to convince myself that I was a sophisticated, complex guy having a profound experience — not just a guy poisoning his own liver.

My need to be the smartest guy in the room extended to every liner note, every guitar riff, and every piece of rock-and-roll trivia I could commit to memory.

If you wanted to debate me on it…
You were going to lose.
Not because I was right.
Because I was relentless.

* * *

Because, again, if I was right about the music…
and I was right about the gin…
Then I was in control of my life.

* * *

That was the story.

* * *

So let's talk about what "real music" actually is.
I enjoy music…
but not as much as some people.
My wife, for example.

* * *

One night we were sitting on the couch watching *The Voice* or *American Idol*—I honestly don't remember which—when she turned to me and asked:

"If you could only choose one for the rest of your life—music or movies—what would it be?"

Without hesitation, I said, "Movies."

I've always loved movies. As a kid, I wanted to be an actor.

She didn't even pause.

"Music. Without a doubt."

She started talking about the emotional connection music creates—how it shapes memories, how it becomes the soundtrack to your life.

She's younger than I am. She grew up on nineties pop, grunge, rap, and hip-hop. Not exactly my lane at the time.

But I've come around on some of it.

I enjoy Snoop Dogg. Tupac was a true artist.

Those guys—and many others—didn't just make music.

They moved culture.

It's funny.

When hip-hop first hit, people called it antisocial.

But a lot of it carried some of the most important social messages of its time.

Unfortunately, a lot of that depth got buried under the whole "men being men" thing—chest-puffing, ego, competition, the constant need to prove who was bigger, better, stronger.

Sound familiar?

*　*　*

We are animals at our core.

Not gentlemen.

But we can be trained.

By ourselves.

By our loved ones.

Or by life, when it finally hits hard enough.

Music as a Reflection of Time

Music has always been a mirror of the era it comes from.

The sunshine of the 1940s.

The birth of rock and roll in the 1950s.

The rebellion of the 1960s.

Disco and pop in the 1970s.

And then… hip-hop.

*　*　*

Much like rock and roll, hip-hop faced resistance.

People feared it.

Fought it.

Tried to shut it down.

But change was coming, and music carried it forward anyway.

And whether people want to admit it or not, I think we're a more tolerant, more connected society because of it.

* * *

There are so many great artists in the world, I couldn't possibly make a dent in a true "all-time great" list without turning this into a completely different book.

And that's not what this is.

I'm not writing the Big Book of Music.

I'm writing about how I thought about music.

Which, at the time…

was a problem.

* * *

So here's a random list of artists I love:

Train, Cher (yeah, I said it), ABBA, Aerosmith, Sinatra, Patti Page, Gaga, Kenny Chesney, Bon Jovi, The Eagles, Led Zeppelin, Streisand, Dean Martin, Adam Lambert, Carrie Underwood, Reba, Elton John, Michael Jackson, Prince, George Michael, Zac Brown Band, Bob Marley, David Bowie, Pink, Neil Diamond.

You're free to disagree.

Just keep it to yourself.

This is my book.

* * *

But here's where it gets serious.

My top tier.

MEAT LOAF – A TRUE ONE-OF-A-KIND

Meat Loaf was… well, Meat Loaf—and I loved everything about this over-the-top, mega-macho emotional performer.

He didn't just sing songs—he performed emotional epics. He was a rock singer with the soul of a Broadway lead, belting out teenage dreams and midlife crises like they were life-or-death operas. Every track felt like a three-act play, complete with heartbreak, thunder, and the occasional baseball commentary. Where other rock stars gave you riffs and attitude, Meat Loaf gave you a show. It wasn't just music—it was theater with a backbeat.

To drive the point home, he recorded more than eight songs, each with a runtime of over eight minutes. Yes, his songs were epically long. He didn't care about radio edits or short attention spans. He cared about telling the whole damn story. *Bat Out of Hell* wasn't just an album—it was a ride, crashing through love, loss, lust, and resurrection. "I'd Do Anything for Love (But I Won't Do That)" still confuses people, and that's part of the magic. He left space for drama, mystery, and pure, over-the-top passion.

Meat Loaf was never cool in the usual way—and thank God for that.

He even had a scene-stealing role in *The Rocky Horror Picture Show,* and the cast really ate him up. And just when you thought he couldn't surprise you anymore, he showed up in *Fight Club* as Robert Paulson—a gentle soul with a tragic story, wrapped in the body of a man with "bitch tits" and a heart too big for that world. In a film full of chaos and anger, Meat Loaf brought something rare:

warmth.

I'll use Meat Loaf's own song titles to toast him: as I sit and think about Meat Loaf, "It's All Coming Back to Me Now" (a Meat Loaf—not a Celine Dion—song!). He was truly a "Bat Out of Hell," looking back at "Objects in the Rear View Mirror..." where "Rock and Roll Dreams Come Through," and he was always willing to "Lie for You" in "Paradise by the Dashboard Light." When he passed away, there was "Not a Dry Eye Left in the House." Lastly, he was a "Dead Ringer for Love" and had a "Hot Patootie"—bless his soul.

Elvis – The Meteor That Changed Everything

Elvis didn't just change music.

He changed religion. He changed culture. He changed American life.

This small-town country boy became the brightest star of his time—maybe the brightest ever. He gave us a new way to worship, a new way to move, a new way to be.

I could write an entire book about Elvis, but I can't because I don't know anything about him that hasn't already been said. Over 400 books and 100 movies have been made about The King, not including the 31 studio movies he starred in.

But Elvis was also trapped and tortured by a man who gained control of him, and The King was powerless against The Colonel.

And that part still pisses me off.

Imagine what he could have done if he had been truly free —free from manipulation, free to follow his own path.

Unmanageable.

That is the word used to describe our lives before we joined AA.

We were trapped by booze.

Elvis was trapped by a cunning, baffling, powerful man.

This man manipulated Elvis's brain, and it translated into Elvis's actions. With the Colonel in charge, Elvis was successful —like a high-functioning alcoholic—but eventually, he hit rock bottom. When he realized he didn't need the Colonel in his life (just like saying, I don't need to drink today), he was reborn and enjoyed a career resurgence.

Unfortunately, the damage was done.

The Colonel had taken the best of Elvis, and he died way too young.

I was not old enough to see Elvis in his heyday, but my mom loved him.

Loved him.

She collected plates—which was a big deal in the seventies —and had over a hundred of them. Some were still in boxes that were never even opened. Of those plates, she had multiples of Elvis. I saw them every day of my life growing up. They were on the walls of our living room.

The first and most heard album of my youth was an Elvis album. I don't remember the songs, but I remember the cover— Elvis off to the side, wearing a cowboy hat, smiling, with a bright blue sky behind him.

My mom wept—no, she bawled—the day Elvis died, and for many days after.

It was hard to watch.

I didn't understand it then.

I do now.

And knowing what I know about the Colonel…

There is a special place in hell for that man.

Toby Keith – A True American Badass

I smile whenever I hear Toby Keith.

His music is just plain fun. "Red Solo Cup" and "I Love This Bar" are anthems for enjoying life and drinking too much. And yes—as a recovering alcoholic—I can still find the humor and the good times in those songs. People who are not addicts should enjoy a party, as long as it's done safely.

One of his songs, "Rum is the Reason," is a total rant about how booze diminishes our potential—sung in a way that is anything but preachy.

That's talent.

This guy sang about giving beer to his horses while his men enjoyed whiskey. His patriotic songs hit me every time. "Call a Marine" is an upbeat tribute to the get-it-done attitude of the American military. "American Soldier" is a tear-jerker. And when "Courtesy of the Red, White, and Blue" comes on, I sit up straighter and start singing like an idiot.

It's like the Rocky theme playing in my head.

Only this time, it's about real people. Real sacrifice. Real loss.

Sadly, Toby Keith passed peacefully on February 5th, 2024, surrounded by his family.

Cheers to you, Toby.

A true American original.

Harry Chapin – The Storyteller That Tried to Cure Hunger

I have to give a nod to Harry Chapin.

His music entered my life when I was in junior high school. I was fourteen years old, and my teacher played a song about a mass-murdering sniper to demonstrate what loneliness and isolation can turn into.

At the time, it was just a story.

Now, it's something I see every day.

Fifty years later, I sit in rooms with people suffering from alcoholism—a disease that, unchecked, leads to that exact same loneliness and isolation.

The song is "Sniper." It's based on a true story and was featured on an album called *Sniper and Other Love Songs.*

Other love songs?

More like songs about people who never felt it.

If "Sniper" doesn't give you chills, and "A Better Place to Be" doesn't bring a tear to your eye, you might be made of stone.

I've had a lifelong dream of turning "A Better Place to Be" into a screenplay. I want John Goodman or Danny DeVito as the little man, Jennifer Aniston as the woman, and Melissa McCarthy as the waitress. If you steal that idea, send royalties.

Harry's music touches something deep in me.

But here's the part that matters more now than it did then:

He wasn't just writing songs.

He was feeding the world.

Before it was trendy. Before it was branding. Before people made careers out of "doing good."

He just did it.

He stayed after his shows until every autograph was signed. He lived simply. And when he died in a car accident on July 16, 1981, he was driving a 1975 Volkswagen Rabbit.

He had no money to speak of.

Because he gave it away.

Harry fed the world—with food and with stories.

MY TWO FAVORITES: QUEEN & JIMMY BUFFETT – AN UNLIKELY PAIR

I know, I know—Queen and Jimmy Buffett together as my top picks? It might make your head spin. But hear me out. Freddie Mercury and Jimmy Buffett had one major thing in common: they didn't follow trends. They created them. Queen fused opera, soul, ballads, and hard rock into something completely unique. Jimmy and the Coral Reefers built an entire subculture of beach life with a country twist.

Both artists defined a lifestyle.

JIMMY BUFFETT – THE POET OF THE BEACH

Jimmy's biggest hit, "Margaritaville," started a lifestyle for countless Parrot Heads. Jimmy had been out at sea, and when he finally got back to land, he was starving and ate a cheeseburger. He was so excited about it, he wrote "Cheeseburger in Paradise." Being that cheeseburgers are one of my favorite pleasures, I totally relate.

Jimmy wrote the hit "Let's Get Drunk" (better known by its full title, "Let's Get Drunk and Screw"). At the time, that was a very provocative title and subject for a song. Interestingly, though, he penned the song under the name Marvin Gardens. I guess he didn't want blowback for his other popular songs. Yes, Marvin Gardens is a tribute to the board game Monopoly. The question is, did Jimmy ever screw at Marvin Gardens?

Jimmy is also credited for writing "It's 5 O'Clock Somewhere," but he only wrote a small portion of it. Jim Brown and Don Rollins really wrote the song, and Alan Jackson recorded it. It has become a worldwide call to party. The success of that song demonstrates Jimmy's love of collaboration. He shared the stage with everyone from The Eagles to Jon Bon Jovi, to Zac Brown, to Kermit the Frog (yes, really).

One of my favorite Jimmy stories involves his longtime friend Glenn Frey of The Eagles. Jimmy had been out on tour, and when he came home, Glenn told him that his assistant had taken one of Jimmy's cars for a joyride. The car ended up in a ditch—or maybe a swimming pool, depending on who's telling it. Instead of getting pissed, Jimmy did what Jimmy did—he wrote a song about it. That song? "Gypsies in the Palace." Now that's how you handle a situation.

Jimmy's first hit was "Come Monday" in 1974, but for me, the song that got me hooked was "Margaritaville." That little beach song was playing on the radio one day when I was leaving my dying mother's bedside. The song lifted my spirits and told me to take it easy. That frozen concoction did help me hold on during a very tough time. Of course, now I know there were better ways than drinking to cope with my mom's upcoming death, but searching for comfort, Margaritaville Radio became the weekend music staple at our house. Today, with no alcohol in my life, I still celebrate the Margaritaville lifestyle. I honestly wouldn't change it, even if I could.

I heard "A Pirate Looks at Forty" a thousand times before AA and never realized how much the song mirrors a 12-step journey:

- "I have been drunk now for over two weeks." *Classic alcoholic admission.*
- "I passed out, and I rallied, and I sprung a few leaks" *Relapse, mistakes, the whole cycle.*
- "Got to stop wishin', got to go fishin'" *Action over wishful thinking—exactly what we say in AA.*
- "Down to rock bottom again, just a few friends" *Most alcoholics have to hit bottom before they get help. And you NEED friends to stay sober.*

It's funny how music takes on a whole new meaning when you hear it through the lens of sobriety.

Freddie Mercury & Queen – A Personal Reflection

I remember the first time I heard Queen—it was at a handbell festival around 1975. This was a gathering of mostly "good church folks" who came together to worship and ring bells. It was a very tame event. Christian boys and girls bashfully asking each other to dance. I emphasize the Christianity of it all because, honestly, who else but church types get together to ring bells for fun?

Then, out struts this guy in tights and a fur wrap onto the stage, and pre-recorded music starts playing. This crazy character started lip-syncing to "Bohemian Rhapsody." I had never heard the song before. I remember thinking: What kind of crazy bull-shit is this? And more importantly, how the hell did the Christians let this nutball perform for us pure-as-the-driven-snow teenagers?

But then, I actually listened to the music. I turned to my older brother and asked, What is this? He told me, That's Queen. That rocked my naïve little world. A few days later, I heard the song on the radio. I was hooked.

I loved Queen's music so much that I convinced my mom to get us tickets to see them at The Fabulous Forum in Los Angeles. To this day, it's the best time I've ever had with my clothes on. Freddie's voice was insane. I was on cloud nine for months afterward. I wanted to be Freddie. I remember taking my Hai-Karate cologne bottle and attaching it to my brother's guitar stand to make a replica of Freddie's boom mic.

My Favorite Queen Songs:

- SOMEBODY TO LOVE: Hands down, one of the greatest songs ever written. The original recording is the standard by which I judge all other songs.

- WE WILL ROCK YOU & WE ARE THE CHAMPIONS: A gay lead singer recording and performing two songs that still rock the most macho sporting events around the world.

- THE SHOW MUST GO ON: The bravery of Freddie is on full display. He was dying, and he still delivered one of the most powerful vocal performances in rock history.

- I Want to Break Free: The video had the band dressing in drag—so far ahead of its time.

- Crazy Little Thing Called Love: This song holds a special place in my heart—it was the song my wife and I had the DJ play as we left our wedding reception to go shoot pool in our formal attire. (Side note: Years before our wedding, Missy and I's first kiss was at the same pool hall. We smashed our teeth together. Ouch!)

Queen + Adam Lambert

I've seen Queen with Paul Rodgers, but when Adam Lambert stepped in as frontman, everything clicked. The first time I saw Adam perform with Queen, he stopped and spoke to the audience: "I know what you're thinking. 'He is no Freddie Mercury.' Hell no, I'm not! There was only one fucking Freddie Mercury, and I miss him too. It is an honor to play with these guys and sing these songs. Sit back and enjoy the show."

That level of respect for Freddie is genuine. Freddie Mercury kicked down the doors for so many artists who came after him. Would there have been an Adam Lambert without Freddie? Of course. But Freddie did it first—and he did it in a big, bold, unapologetic way.

My fierce defense of Adam actually goes all the way back to his time on American Idol. I remember watching his season and being absolutely blown away by his vocal range. He was a rock god trapped on a pop competition show. When it came down to the finale, he lost to some guy with an acoustic guitar.

I lost my absolute mind.

I was so incredibly angry that I actually picked a massive fight with my wife over it. Missy was trying to be reasonable, pointing out that maybe the other guy just appealed to the show's core demographic. But the guy you are reading about in these early chapters couldn't just have a calm disagreement. I had to be right, and I had to be loud about it.

I started yelling that Adam only lost because Middle America was full of homophobic bigots who couldn't handle voting for a guy wearing eyeliner. I ranted, I raved, and I let my ego turn a television show into a full-blown marital argument. I was an asshole.

But looking back on that ridiculous fight today, it hits me differently. Yes, I was an arrogant jerk about how I delivered the message, but underneath all that bluster, I was genuinely furious at the bigotry I saw playing out on the screen. It's interesting to look back and realize how fiercely I was willing to defend a gay man I had never even met. I didn't fully understand why that specific injustice struck such a deep, personal nerve in me back then. I just knew it was wrong.

I remember an interview where Freddie was asked what he thought would happen after he died. His response? "I want to go to hell. That's where all the interesting people are." Classic Freddie.

The Final Sad Similarity

There's a heartbreaking connection between Jimmy Buffett and Freddie Mercury: Both died too young, and both from doing what they loved.

Jimmy loved the outdoors. He lived for the beach, the sun, and the boat life. And in the end, he passed from a rare form of skin cancer—a direct result of his love for the sunshine. Freddie loved to party. Let's just say his lifestyle caught up with him. We lost him to complications from AIDS far too soon.

Two legends. Two completely different lives. But both unstoppable forces in music.

When you're sitting on the sand with a drink in your hand, Jimmy is there. When you're singing at the top of your lungs in the car, Freddie is there.

That's the magic of music—it never really dies.

INTERLUDE: The Breakup Letter

AUTHOR'S NOTE: *Before I jump into my next obsession, I need to break character for a second. Looking back at the guy who was fiercely defending his martinis and his music, it's easy to get lost in the trivia and the ego. But underneath all of that noise, a very quiet, terrifying reality was taking hold. While my ego was holding onto the past, my soul was writing a very different kind of letter.*

Goodbye Alcohol,

To you, my old friend. I need to break up with you forever. It's not you, it's me.

Although you hurt me greatly. You literally

broke my liver. It's not your fault. I did the damage. I loved you too much and became obsessed with you. I see now that you have a power over me to take me down dark roads into dangerous places. I refuse to go on that journey with you. The only things I love unconditionally now are my wife and my God.

I wish to release any control you had on me. I'll be honest with you: even though you are cunning, baffling, and powerful, you lose my devotion to you.

We had some great times. You offered me an opportunity to flourish in business and earn a nice income. There were grandiose meals, and sometimes, the meals were magical and memorable. I remember meals enjoyed in caves and smoke-filled restaurants. Now I know the experiences weren't worth the price you charged.

Alcohol, you have also introduced me to friends I will have for life. Great friendships have been made while enjoying your myriad of products. I also met some very smart people. There are Master Sommeliers and Masters of Wine. The people who hold these titles are charming and smart. Most of them, I believe, could be Grand Master Chess players, but instead, they use their powerful minds to learn, teach, and promote wine. I will miss going to wine tastings and dinners hosted by these people, but now I am smart enough to know that if I go to see these Geniuses speak, you alcohol, my crappy, crappy friend, will suck me in for what could literally be my last supper, so I say to you, no way, and fuck off.

I thought it was a fun ride. I was so wrong. You took so much more from me than you gave. You tried to steal my life way too early. I was in arguments with loved ones under your influence. You brought out ugly Bill, and I never want to see that monster again. You cost me memories of great times with family and friends. You made me irritable. You made me spend way too much money on you. You made me waste years I could have been of service to people. You made me more self-centered and ego-driven.

You cost me time with my son. You also took him hostage for years. You came between God and me. Are you Satan or just one of his agents? You made my wife worry she was going to lose me way too early.

I choose life with my AA friends, wife, and God. It was fun but awful to know you so well. With my bible, big book, and sponsor, I will stay recovered from your poisonous grip forever.

Consider yourself ghosted, my old frenemy.

Now I replace you, my spirit demon, with people. People in a beautiful fellowship called Alcoholics Anonymous. They are my family now. I will meet far more interesting people full of love and service than I ever met through you, alcohol. This AA fellowship wants me to be all I can be. The best me. I gladly trade the ancient caves and smoky restaurants for ancient-looking rooms with folding chairs and smoky patios. I give up world-class dining for world-class unity. You alcohol gave me false pleasure, but this new family offers me life and spirituality as I have never known it. You alcohol really have nothing but dead ends to offer me.

Food & Fire

Now that I've gotten that breakup letter off my chest, let's get back to what the old Bill did best: having a loud, uncompromising, and absolutely correct opinion on everything.

If you want to understand how my ego operated, you don't just look at what was in my glass. You look at what was on my plate. I wasn't just a snob about gin; I was a dictator about food. And if there is one culinary hill I am willing to die on, it is this:

I fucking hate chicken.

There are so many things I'd rather eat than chicken. Yes, chicken is good for you. There, I said it. Americans eat more chicken than pork and beef combined, but I still don't want to eat it. It's dry, flavorless, and boring. Chicken is what they serve at weddings because it is never terrible, and not much is expected of it. If you want the food at your wedding to be safe, cheap, and inoffensive, you serve chicken. It's a reliable choice, but reliability doesn't equal excitement. It's just... chicken.

There is a canned tuna product called *Chicken of the Sea.* Why in the hell would you want anything to taste like chicken if it wasn't already chicken? Gross. Chicken noodle soup is fine, I guess, but how does protein in liquid form still manage to be dry? It's a paradox wrapped in disappointment. And why, I ask, would we eat a bird so lame it can't even fly? Ducks fly, and they're delicious. Quail fly, and they're even tastier. Ostriches don't fly, but their massive eggs make up for it. Turkeys? Maybe even worse than chicken, but at least we only have to choke that shit down twice a year. Chicken, however, remains the reigning champion of the yucky protein contest, day in and day out.

And let's talk about the parts of a chicken. The tasty parts— the dark meat—are full of cartilage and other unappealing, chewy bits. The white meat, on the other hand, is about as compelling as eating chalk. Sure, it's lean, packed with protein, but it's also as dry as the Sahara and about as flavorful. Dark meat may taste slightly better, but it has twice the fat and half the protein of white meat. Meanwhile, the breast, the part everyone pushes as the "healthy" choice, is just an obligation on a plate.

Now, I'll admit, there are a few ways to eat chicken that aren't entirely miserable. Mostly, if you want good chicken, move to France. But, if relocation isn't an option, there are a few passable choices here in the U.S.:

- CHICK-FIL-A: This used to be the gold standard for fast-food chicken. It's still good, but others have caught up and, in some cases, surpassed it. Spicy chicken, Nashville hot chicken, Louisiana-style— you name it, someone is doing it better. Chick-fil-A is now the McDonald's of chicken sandwiches. Decent, but not revolutionary. Solid, consistent, but no longer alone at the top.

- COSTCO ROTISSERIE CHICKEN: This is the real deal. Sometimes, it's even great. And with the rotisserie ovens Costco uses costing over $100,000, it damn well should be. There's something about the slow roasting, the self-basting, and the seasoning that makes this one of the few widely available chickens worth eating.

- FRIED CHICKEN: Of course, fried chicken is good. But is it really still chicken once you deep-fry all the dryness out of it and replace it with crispy, juicy, flavorful fat? I mean, I'm not complaining, but at that point, we're really just celebrating batter.

But there is one glorious exception. One poultry dish that stands above the rest.

- CHICKEN CUTLETS (MADE BY MY WIFE, SPECIFICALLY) This is where we move beyond the ordinary and into the divine. My wife makes chicken cutlets that are little works of art. I have had chicken cutlets in some fancy places, and none of them hold a candle to hers. If she were to go on *Beat Bobby Flay*, she'd leave that man in a smoldering pile of culinary defeat. He could bring all the crispy rice, Calabrian chili, and Iron Chef, TV-star techniques he wanted—she'd still mop the floor with him.

Her cutlets are perfection. No secrets, no weird spices, no forced-in dark meat—just pure, old-fashioned, thin-pounded chicken breast. Egg wash, seasoned breadcrumbs, and a perfect pan-fry. The result? A golden, deep brown crust, flecked with lighter specks of crispiness. There are even a few spots that are slightly darker, adding an intensity of flavor that rivals a perfectly grilled steak. These deep brown pockets flirt with the edge of bitterness, stopping just before the precipice, staying sweet, savory, and crisp.

When her cutlets hit the plate, they shine. Not greasy, just kissed with a sheen of perfection—like the pavement after a May morning drizzle. The crunch is audible. Your knife glides through, revealing tender, moist chicken beneath the crust. The scent is intoxicating—warm toasted olive oil, fresh baked bread, a hint of garlic, and herbs.

Then, the first bite.

Your taste buds skip a beat, stunned by the sheer glory of this chicken. It's like gazing at the Mona Lisa for the first time —there's a physical reaction, an involuntary recognition of something special. The toasted breadcrumbs adhere to the chicken in perfect unison, the olive oil imparts richness without heaviness, and the texture is just right—substantial without being tough, tender without being mushy. Each bite is a symphony.

And just when you think it can't get better, she serves it with pesto pasta. Let me be clear: I love pesto pasta. But when my wife makes chicken cutlets, I eat every last piece of chicken before touching the pasta. And that's saying something.

It's not just about the taste. It's about the care, the love, the attention to detail. She knows I hate chicken, and yet she takes the time to make it so perfect that even I can't resist it. That, right there, is love.

THE MASTER LIST

Because my ego required me to be the authority on all things culinary, I didn't just have opinions on chicken. I had a curated mental map of the greatest foods on earth. Here are my absolute favorites, in no particular order:

- IN-N-OUT BURGER DOUBLE-DOUBLE: Don't get a single. One patty throws off the balance of the bun and meat. It has to be a Double-Double, even if you only eat half of it.

- THE HICKORY BURGER AT APPLE PAN (WEST LA): Classic Americana. Just a bench full of people, nothing fancy. You will love it or hate it. My wife is on the hate side. She is WRONG!

- STEAK: Pretty much any way, as long as it's not overcooked. I make a mean steak on my grill, on The Big Green Egg, or pan-fried once in a while. Few restaurants compare to what my friends Dave, Nick, and I can do with a steak.

- OYSTERS: Damn it, all the way to hell. I had to give these beautiful little sea creatures up when I got a new liver—something about bacteria, blah, blah, blah. I listened to the doctors on this one (I should have listened to the first time they told me my liver was in trouble). These briny little gems are so tasty. I loved them with martinis.

- UNI WITH A QUAIL EGG: Yet another food I had to give up with this new liver. This was always my last bite of sushi. Uni, if you don't know, is sea urchin. Once, I was at my local hole-in-the-wall sushi place by the ocean, and some guys had just caught fresh uni. They traded it with the owner for dinner. Best uni ever.

- PIZZA: Pizza runs the gamut from shitty to life-changing. That frozen one with the tagline 'It's not delivery'—yeah, I have eyes, I can see your crappy pizza on TV. Chicago pizza? Overrated. New York pizza? Pretty good. But the best pizza I've ever had? Tony's in San Francisco, hands down. Tony Gemignani has won multiple World's Best Pizza awards, and his place has four different pizza ovens, each dedicated to a specific style.

- FRESH WARM DONUTS: My favorite is the apple fritter. It just so happened that the time I had to drop my son off at daycare was the exact same time the donut shop across the street was frying apple fritters. When I bit into it, I was stunned. I had no idea a donut could be so much better just by being warm.

- PINK'S HOT DOGS: A Hollywood legend for a good reason. I used to go weekly when it was in my territory—never waited more than 10 minutes. Now, thanks to TV food shows, it is an hour or more wait.

While we are on the subject of hot dogs, I need to lay down an absolute, unbending culinary law. If you are over the age of eight, you do not put ketchup on a hot dog. Ever.

Whether you are eating a "dirty water dog" from a cart in New York City or a beautifully constructed Chicago dog, ketchup is a crime against encased meats. The former president of Vienna Beef actually wrote a book where he talked about this.

It became a regular thing to have hot dogs at the owner's house for the President of the United States. One time, a Secret Service guy asked for ketchup, and the President looked at him and told his detail, "If I don't get ketchup, neither do you." *That* is a true patriot.

Honestly, if you are a parent and you let your kid put ketchup on a hot dog, you are failing your child and setting them up for a lifetime of culinary mediocrity. Mustard, onions, relish, chili, cheese—all acceptable. Ketchup? Grow up.

Back to Pink's, I have to share this story.

One time, I was working with the owner of one of the wineries I represented. In that biz, we call them "work-withs." The sales rep (me) takes the winery owner to see accounts and gives buyers the story straight from the horse's mouth.

On this particular glorious, sunny, 75-degree day, we were working just outside Beverly Hills. I asked the owner if he wanted a quick lunch or a long, fancy food experience. He chose quickly. I said, "Pink's it is." He was excited because he had heard about this famous hot dog joint.

Pink's is literally a shack standing on La Brea Boulevard at Melrose in the heart of Hollywood. Its location is a Southern California cliché. Bums and homeless people on the sidewalks while Rolls-Royces and Ferraris roll down the street. Beautiful people everywhere. People talking to themselves. Think Eddie Murphy as Axel Foley in *Beverly Hills Cop*.

We waited in line for about thirty minutes—enough time to see half a dozen hookers, and at least two drug deals go down. I asked the owner, who was about 6 inches shorter and 100 pounds lighter than I, what he wanted. A double or a single? He asked me what I was having and said he would just have the same.

I looked at him with astonishment. What I order is not for the faint of heart, and certainly not for a first-time Pink's customer. He was a small fry, but he was paying, so what the fuck. Just before we got to the front, I asked him a third time if he was sure. A resounding "Hell yes" was the response.

I ordered two "Bacon Burrito Dogs." A Bacon Burrito Dog is two foot-long hot dogs with onions, cheese, and six pieces of bacon, smothered in chili and wrapped in a giant flour tortilla. In addition, I ordered two chili cheese fries and four cream sodas (two for each of us).

We took the food to the patio and sat in the shade. After his first bite, I asked, "How's the dog?" He said it was delicious and kept eating. But about halfway through his burrito and a few fries into his belly, he looked at me, as white as a ghost with a slightly green tint, and said, "I'm done."

I gave him a comforting look and said, "Let me finish up, and we will start seeing more accounts."

He let out a slight burp and said, "No, I am done for the day. Take me to my hotel when you are done."

Let this be a lesson: When you visit someone's hood, listen to their shit!

Fire & The Outdoor Kitchen

A true food dictator needs a proper domain, and I'm lucky enough to have a decent outdoor kitchen. While my equipment is top-notch, the space itself is a little thrown together. It doesn't light up like a major league stadium, but it's plenty bright when you need it.

The centerpiece is my 54-inch Lynx grill. Let me tell you, it is the pinnacle of outdoor cooking gear. It has three regular burners and a high-heat sear unit, and it's so big that when it arrived, we almost needed a crane to get it through the side walkway. Honestly, I could cook eight whole prime ribs on it at once.

To the left of the grill is a palm tree atrium, and in front of that sits my Kamado Big Green Egg. It's an amazing appliance—smoker, grill, oven—all in one. My favorite thing to make in it is a chocolate chip cookie pie. On the far left, I have my Ooni pizza oven. A pompous, bespoke brand from Michigan sells a similar oven for $12,000. Mine? I paid $600 for it, and it makes just as good (if not better) pizza. My Ooni sits on a $25 table I picked up at a discount furniture store, but it works perfectly.

Now, let me say a quick word about grilling vs. BBQ. In California, we tend to think everything cooked outside is grilled. But grilling involves high, direct or indirect heat, while BBQ is a slower process over lower heat. Smoking is a subset of BBQ with very low heat over a long period—think brisket or pulled pork.

When it comes to steaks, I often use the reverse sear

method. Instead of searing the steak at high heat first, you cook it slowly over low heat, adding smoke flavor and locking in juices. Once it's about 80% done, you crank up the heat and sear it. It goes against what most of us "Men" learned about cooking a steak, but it works beautifully.

My favorite use of my outdoor kitchen is entertaining. If we have a big crowd on the Fourth of July, I fire up the Green Egg the night before and put a pork butt on around 2:00 AM. The smoke does its magic while I sleep. Meanwhile, the pizza oven is cranking out pizzas, and on the Lynx grill, I'm flipping burgers and grilling hot dogs.

Of course, with all that food and drink flowing, not everything always goes smoothly. One year, we had a dozen people from the wine business at our party. With so many pros around, Missy and I decided to open a six-liter bottle (equivalent to eight standard bottles) of a very good wine left over from our wedding.

There was plenty of hoopla over this legendary, aged wine being opened. We gave everyone actual wine glasses—no red solo cups for us. Someone inserted the corkscrew, pulled... and the corkscrew came out clean. The cork stayed in the bottle, now with a hole right through the center.

Son of a bitch. This was a mess. A bottle that heavy with a loose cork would spell disaster.

"Shit," I thought. "I gotta do something." I grabbed a second corkscrew. My friend Nick and I put both corkscrews into separate locations in the giant cork.

Someone yelled, "Have you ever done this before?"

"No fucking way," I said, thinking this will never work, and we are going to have to decant this giant bitch. But I was already half drunk, so...

"One. Two."

Another yell from the crowd: "Is this on YouTube?"

"Three." Nick and I pulled.

Miraculously, the massive cork came out clean with perfect staining, like a video shoot. It was perfect. We did good. The wine was delicious, and we finished the bottle. I just wish we were smart enough to get a video. Now it just lives on in our memories. A legendary story to be passed on.

I love cooking outside, and no matter how great the setup, the equipment, or the food, it's the people I share it with that make it special.

ACT II: SURRENDER TO THE UNMANAGEABLE

The Obligatory Alcoholic Rant

If you made it through my rants about martinis, music, and chicken without throwing this book across the room, congratulations. You now have a very clear picture of exactly who I was. But ego can only take you so far. Eventually, the universe steps in and forces you to surrender.

For me, that surrender began in the hospital.

When you have the disease—and alcoholism is a disease—it's almost impossible to quit drinking without help. The American Medical Association defines alcoholism as "a disease characterized by impaired control over alcohol consumption, leading to detrimental effects on an individual's health, interpersonal relationships, and social/economic functioning". This definition emphasizes the compulsive nature of alcohol use despite adverse consequences.

The care team at the hospital was a godsend. That wonderful organization was Kaiser Permanente. FYI, "permanente" is a Latin word meaning "lasting". When I learned that Kaiser was a nonprofit organization, I couldn't believe it. According to their website, they are the country's largest private nonprofit healthcare organization, providing care for 12.5 million Americans. Sometimes, KP gets a bad rap for long wait times and a somewhat old-school approach. But in my experience, there are no better caregivers on the planet than the Kaiser team when it comes to treating chemical dependency.

A God Moment & Green Gowns

One morning in the hospital, I was staring out the window at the hills when I heard a knock on my door and two voices saying, "We're from St. Someone's Church for the Archdiocese of Los Angeles". *Holy Shit!* Was I receiving last rites? Nope. They just wanted me to know they'd be praying for me. That was the exact moment I knew I'd do whatever it took to stay sober. I'll call that a God Moment.

One of the unexpected benefits of being in the hospital was discovering how much love and concern my friends and family had for me. My best friend lives about fifty miles away from the hospital, but he made the trip several times—and in L.A. traffic, that's a *real* commitment. His brother, another close friend, also visited. One day, all three of us were in my hospital room. I was wearing that ridiculous gown in that oddly specific shade of hospital green. Green gowns, green trays, green scrubs. Did a study prove that dying people respond best to green?

There we were, three guys hanging out, me in my drafty little gown, but I wasn't embarrassed. Normally, I'd feel awkward, maybe even self-conscious, but with these guys, I felt comfortable. Safe. We laughed. I don't remember what we talked about (thanks, foggy brain), but I know it was fun. And for the first time in a while, I thought, I'm going to be okay. I'm getting out of here.

I've known those guys for over fifty years, and I thank God they're in my life. We met when we all sang in the church choir. Well, *they* sang. I can't carry a tune to save my life; I just made loud noises, and they were kind enough to tolerate it. Back in the day, we were also part of an all-male handbell choir. Yeah, handbells. And believe it or not, we were *good*. Years later, when I was running a restaurant and raising my son in Oregon, the bell choir played at the Pope's Masses at Dodger Stadium and the Coliseum in L.A. An actual performance for the Pope, while I was across state lines, missing out. In Oregon, I wrote my first wine list and unlocked a deep love for alcohol that grew into something much bigger and much darker over time. It didn't hit all at once, but that's when it started. Funny that they teach kids about safe sex in school, but not about the dangers of alcohol for those predisposed to addiction.

COMING HOME TO A SOBER HOUSE

While I was in the hospital, my wife arranged for friends to clear out all the alcohol—almost *all* of it. We kept a few very expensive collectible bottles and have them to this day, against the advice of my therapist. I came home to my couch, my bed, my TV, my clothes, and our puppies. But the booze was gone. For the first time, I would be sober *alone*.

My wonderful wife travels for work. When she left on her first business trip after I got home, a friend stepped in. He's a chef, one of the few men I can say *"I love you"* to without it being weird. He stayed a few nights and came over every day for a week, making sure I was okay. And, let me tell you, he *cooked*. I thought I'd died and gone to heaven. For the first time in my life, I had an endless supply of great food, and none of it was green. One morning, he made an egg salad sandwich, and suddenly, I was a kid again. It tasted like childhood. At that moment, I realized I'd been given a second chance at life. I'd been *reborn*. I had to be on a low-sodium diet, which meant one of a chef's go-to ingredients was off the table. But he worked around it, and everything he made was incredible. We watched a lot of football. One random Tuesday night in October, he found a college game for us to watch. I had no idea football was on TV on Tuesday nights, but if you look hard enough, you can find it.

A Different Kind of Thanksgiving

That Thanksgiving, for the first time since childhood, I didn't drink. It was also the first holiday season when I felt truly thankful—not just for the usual things but for life itself. I had so much to be thankful for. I was alive and on a path to living my best life. Sorry to sound like a hippy; I'm sure it won't be the last time.

Thanksgiving has always been a big deal at our house, but the past few years have been bittersweet. In March 2020, we lost my wife's dad, Russ. Thanksgiving was Russ's holiday, his time to shine. His recipes were written out on note cards, and no one could touch the stuffing or gravy. Those were his to make. One year, he spent all day making tamales. We were so full by the time they were ready, no one ate them. He didn't care; he was proud of the work.

The morning of Thanksgiving, he'd wake up early to make Swedish pancakes from a recipe he found in the classic *Joy of Cooking* by Irma Rombauer. A few years ago, I started making breakfast sausages to go with the pancakes. At first, Russ wasn't on board—*not tradition!*—but eventually, he came around. After pancakes, he'd start mixing Ramos Gin Fizzes (recipe in *San Francisco à la Carte*). In 2023, we made them *virgins*. Big change? Yes, but they tasted *damn* good. And more importantly, they weren't a trigger. A *trigger* is something that gives an alcoholic the intense urge to drink. Science now understands that these cravings are more than a lack of willpower; an alcoholic's brain is wired differently. It craves, fights, and *demands* a drink.

Luckily, the virgin Ramos Gin Fizz didn't stir that beast in me. It was just… a drink.

When I was newly sober, four of my relatives from Texas stayed with us for Thanksgiving week—David, his wife Kathy, and their two kids. We wondered if I'd be up for it, but it turned out to be a blessing. They're relatives through marriage, but family and friends through love. Kathy and David make you believe in good parenting. They remind me of the Huxtables—fun, loving, but no-nonsense. One minute, their son James was cracking fart jokes with his mom, and the next, she told him to do something. No backtalk, no attitude—just "*Yes, ma'am,*" and it was done. If those two could parent the world, we'd all be better off.

For most of my life, saying grace at Thanksgiving annoyed the shit out of me. I was pretty sure God didn't want us eating cold food. We'd worked hard to get everything on the table—so let's eat! A few times, we went around and had everyone say what they were thankful for. I *hated* that. Now I can't wait to hear everyone's gratitude. That year, I realized we should pray *before* we started plating dinner. AA meetings often close with the Lord's Prayer, and I figured, why not bring that into Thanksgiving? I asked my nieces and nephews to gather every-one, and about fifteen of us stood around my couch while I was still recovering. Together, we said the Lord's Prayer. Four words say it all: *"Thy will be done"*. As we prayed, I thought about the family we'd lost. Of course, I missed them. But more than anything, I felt grateful for the beautiful family I *still* had around me.

The Biker Gang: A Road Trip Cracked Open the Door

To truly understand this newfound gratitude, you have to understand how hard I fought against surrender. A few years before the "idiot doctors" told me I was an alcoholic, I'd tested the AA waters. My brother had recently passed away from a heart attack at fifty-nine, I drank even more from the grief, and for a brief moment, I thought maybe I should cut back. I was driving to the San Fernando Valley, seventy-five miles from my home, to meet with the two brothers I'd hired to handle his estate sale.

It was a typical sunny day in Southern California, and as I drove, I was listening to "Margaritaville," making the trip more pleasant than painful. I arrived early at their headquarters, and I had to kill time, so I went into an antique shop across the parking lot. (A clerk in an airport shop once asked if she could help me. When I said, "I'm just killing time," she gasped, "Oh, honey, don't say that. We have so little time. Don't kill what little you've got"). The antique shop was a strange place, very dimly lit and chilly with antiques and junk galore. After looking at some of the "treasures," I headed back to the estate warehouse with visions of the giant stuffed clowns and Elvis memorabilia I'd just seen floating in my head.

The warehouse was like a time machine. If the antique place smelled like an old house, this place almost smelled like a morgue. It was dingy, with dusty floors and old stuff everywhere I looked. The bookshelves were covered in dust, and the tools for sale were old and rusty. One of the brothers came over in a plaid shirt and said "hello" in a very gravelly voice, which I assumed was from years of smoking. He asked how I was doing, which I thought was a dumb question. My brother had just died in his sleep. How the hell did he think I was doing? We covered the necessities, and we parted ways.

Back on the road with Margaritaville playing, I thought about the drinking lifestyle and decided I should have a margarita. Then I thought, maybe I should use my brother's death as a springboard to drink less. I decided to check out this AA thing instead of the Mexican restaurant. I looked up AA meetings on my phone and found one down the street, which I thought was incredibly lucky. I had no idea you had to want to stop drinking completely to be a member. I thought you could just drink less with their help. (If you want to drink less or taper off, you can contact a medical team called "Harm Reduction." Not AA).

I never made it out of the car. People say they put off AA because they're afraid to share their experiences or don't want to admit they have a problem. For me, it was the people outside the meeting. They scared the shit out of me. I pulled up at what looked like a homeless encampment. They were all smoking and drinking coffee from white Styrofoam cups. Most of them had beards and not the well-trimmed South Orange County beards that gentlemen and hipsters wear, but long, straggly beards. They seemed to be a street gang. Bikers, hoodies, tattoos, hairy arms, muscles—and those were the women. (That joke used to be funny before the world got so fucking sensitive.)

I looked at that motley crew and thought, *No f'en way was I going in there*. I told myself they were weird folks and decided I'd take my chances with booze.

Years later, I went back. On my six-month anniversary of sobriety, I shared this exact story at a meeting, and the crowd laughed. I looked around the room, and lots of long-bearded and tattooed people were laughing with me because we had something in common. We all needed to help each other stop drinking. Now I consider those people family. Turns out, I was just like them. We alcoholics, know each other.

They say when two people with broken limbs are at the same party, they somehow find each other. We recovering alcoholics are the same. I can go to just about any city in the world and walk into an AA meeting, and it feels like home. The bond of our mental and spiritual maladies keeps us close, even if we're strangers.

MY HOME GROUP & THE TWELFTH STEP IN ACTION

When I finally got serious, I started shopping around for meetings. I found an early morning AA meeting—7:30 am. To someone who has spent his adult life in the drinking business, that's the crack of dawn. This meeting was held at the city hall. When I went through the double glass doors, I thought it looked like a courtroom. At the front of the room, I saw a long table with high-backed, throne-like chairs and ropes dividing the public from the city council members. Later in my recovery,

I saw that the room was fresh, clean, and well-maintained, with the obligatory Disneyland photo on one wall. In Orange County, the Mouse is everybody's friend.

The room smelled of freshly brewed coffee—a very welcome smell for a drunk in the first weeks of recovery. I was wearing an L.A. Rams sweater, and a gentleman gave me a very warm greeting: "Hello, go Rams". The room was filled with about forty cushioned stackable chairs in neat rows. The gentleman I met when I came in said, "Keep coming back". I didn't know at the time that was an AA thing to say, but I did come back. I decided it was time to get a Big Book, and I asked him about getting one. He came back with a book, put his name and phone number inside, and gave it to me. A few weeks later, I asked him to be my sponsor. He agreed, and I couldn't be happier; he's a supportive mentor and friend. For almost a year, I've served as secretary at that Monday morning meeting. It's my responsibility to make coffee and set up chairs at seven o'clock in the fucking morning. Thanks, John!

Finding sobriety affects your mind and body in several ways. One of them is a condition called "anhedonia," which is described as feeling numb, hopeless, empty or blank. When you drink, your brain creates too much dopamine, so anhedonia is your mind's attempt to bring you back to balance. I was in a group, and our therapist was talking about anhedonia. One of the group members said she suffered from it and was worried it wouldn't go away. Another member said that trips to Mexico used to bring her great joy, but she'd been unable to experience that in sobriety until one day when she saw the beauty of the hills, trees, and ocean and it was like a switch had been flicked on. She assured her fellow group members that it does, indeed, get better. That was the twelfth step in action, fully realized and on display for the eighteen people in that Zoom meeting. One person helping another.

A NEW KIND OF PRAYER LIFE

In AA, we talk about a Higher Power, but you can call it whatever you like and understand it however you want. Or nothing at all. Another big change is the way I pray. I don't remember a time when I *didn't* pray. When I was a kid, I heard a priest say, "All for the love of you, my God". It sounded cool, so I started saying it. When I got sober, I realized that was bullshit. In the *Big Book*, it says, "We are not saints. The point is that we are willing to grow along spiritual lines". A much more *doable* truth for me? "Thy will be done". For non-believers, that translates to "Whatever will be, will be".

What I *pray for* has changed, too. I used to ask God for things. For outcomes. Now I say, "Thy will be done... and if that happens, if I could include my wife closing a big piece of business, that'd be great". One thing I always pray for is peace and serenity for the families of organ donors. They don't know me, and I don't know them, but I owe them everything. Their loss is my second chance.

I still say prayers from the *Big Book* and from church. The *Serenity Prayer* is a twenty-five-word powerhouse that has saved *countless* lives. Let's break it down:

- *God, grant me the serenity to accept the things I cannot change.* Religious or not, who *doesn't* want serenity?
- *The courage to change the things I can.* You don't need God to decide you want to change. It just takes courage, and we can find that in ourselves.
- *And the wisdom to know the difference.* Wisdom isn't handed down from the heavens; it's learned.

It's *beautiful* that one of the most important prayers in sobriety can be completely God-centered *or* fully secular. Even an atheist can use the *Serenity Prayer* without compromising their beliefs.

AA Jargon & The Promises

Recovery has its own language. If you hang around the barbershop long enough, you'll get a haircut (meaning, show up at meetings again and again). Here is a quick crash course in AA Jargon:

- ONE DAY AT A TIME: We can't think of never drinking again, but we can think of not drinking today.

- ARE YOU A FRIEND OF BILL W?: A way to address a possible member of the family in public.

- BIG BOOK: The official title is *Alcoholics Anonymous: The Story of How More Than One Hundred Men Have Recovered from Alcoholism.*

- BIRTHDAYS: Your Birthday is your sobriety date. We call your birth date your belly button birthday.

- CHIPS: Tokens awarded for periods of sobriety.

- DRY DRUNK: Not drinking or drugging but not working any program to stay sober.

- THREE LEGACIES, THREE PILLARS: Recovery, Service, Unity.

- PROGRESS, NOT PERFECTION: Refers to our inability to live the twelve steps perfectly and reminds us we are only human.

- H.A.L.T.: Hungry, angry, lonely, tired.

- H.O.W.: Honesty, open-mindedness, willingness.

- "I CAN'T, HE CAN, SO I'LL LET HIM": I love this one. It's the first three steps paraphrased.

If you do the work, the Big Book guarantees the NINTH STEP PROMISES:

1. If we are painstaking about this phase of our development, we will be amazed before we are halfway through.
2. We are going to know a new freedom and a new happiness.
3. We will not regret the past nor wish to shut the door on it.
4. We will comprehend the word serenity, and we will know peace.
5. No matter how far down the scale we have gone, we will see how our experience can benefit others.
6. That feeling of uselessness and self-pity will disappear.
7. We will lose interest in selfish things and gain interest in our fellows.
8. Self-seeking will slip away.
9. Our whole attitude and outlook upon life will change.
10. Fear of people and of economic insecurity will leave us.
11. We will intuitively know how to handle situations which used to baffle us.
12. We will suddenly realize that God is doing for us what we could not do for ourselves.

THE PEER COACH CHECK-IN

I want and need to make it crystal clear that any reference to AA in this book is strictly my thoughts and feelings. The book is not affiliated, officially or unofficially, with Alcoholics Anonymous. It's just one man's journey. I called this reflection "Obligatory Alcoholic Rant" because AA teaches us that being of service is the best way to maintain sobriety. I'm obliged to pass on what I've been given.

If your interest was piqued a little or you flinched when you read the title of this reflection, you may benefit from the thoughts below. Sometimes, it's tough to assess your own habits objectively, especially when it comes to drinking. If you've ever wondered about your relationship with alcohol, these questions might help bring clarity:

- HAVE YOU TRIED TO STOP DRINKING FOR A WEEK OR A MONTH, ONLY FOR SOMETHING TO COME UP THAT BREAKS YOUR DRY SPELL? A persistent inability to stay dry can be a red flag.

- DO YOU EVER FEEL JUDGED BY OTHERS FOR YOUR DRINKING? Feeling the need to defend or explain your drinking could suggest you're aware of how it's perceived by others—or perhaps by yourself.

- HAVE YOU SWITCHED DRINKS TO CONSUME LESS ALCOHOL? Changing from high-alcohol drinks to those with lower alcohol content can feel like a compromise, but it might indicate you're attempting to moderate or control your intake.

- HAVE YOU EXPERIENCED ANY PROBLEMS DUE TO DRINKING IN THE PAST YEAR? Financial issues, relationship tension, or trouble at work often creep in when drinking gets out of hand.

- IS YOUR FAMILY LIFE AFFECTED BY YOUR DRINKING? Alcohol use can impact relationships, either through missed family events, arguments, or a growing distance with loved ones.

- DO YOU FIND YOURSELF SEEKING EXTRA DRINKS AT SOCIAL GATHERINGS? Going out of your way to drink more than others or pacing yourself differently from the group can indicate a heavier dependency on alcohol.

- DO YOU TELL YOURSELF YOU CAN STOP ANY TIME, BUT NEVER ACTUALLY TRY? Believing you could stop but not putting it to the test might be a way of avoiding an uncomfortable truth.

- HAVE YOU EVER MISSED OR BEEN LATE TO WORK BECAUSE OF DRINKING OR HANGOVERS? When drinking spills over into your professional life, it's a clear sign that it may be interfering with your responsibilities.

- DO YOU BLACKOUT? Losing chunks of memory after drinking can be dangerous, both for your physical safety and your overall mental health.

- HAVE YOU THOUGHT LIFE WOULD BE BETTER IF YOU DIDN'T DRINK? If you're imagining a happier, healthier life without alcohol, it might be a sign that your drinking is impacting your well-being.

If you answered "yes" to any of these questions, it may be worth exploring what drinking means in your life and whether you want to make a change.

OK, I Have an Alcohol Problem. Now What? If you've come to the point of realizing you have an alcohol problem, you've taken one of the most courageous steps toward change. This admission is no small feat, and recognizing the issue is a powerful first step in moving forward.

In recovery, one of the most valuable pieces of wisdom is that "this is a we program, not a me program". Leaning on others is not a weakness; it's a source of strength. You don't need to carry this alone. It's important to remember that addiction is a disease, not a moral failing. Alcoholism is a complex, progressive disease, but one thing is clear: you are not to blame for having it. However, while you're not at fault, taking responsibility for your recovery and actions is essential.

For alcoholics, "slowing down" or "just drinking less" isn't a long-term solution. Alcoholism is progressive, and over time, it tends to get worse if left unchecked. It's not about willpower; it's about finding the support to stop the cycle. You don't need to lose a job, a relationship, money, or a home before you take action. Waiting for things to hit rock bottom may only make recovery more challenging and the damage more severe. Instead, you can decide today to end the cycle of trying to control or limit your drinking and step into a life where sobriety opens doors to the peace and clarity you deserve.

YOU DON'T HAVE TO DRINK TODAY!

THE BIOLOGICAL COWARD

MY DAD WAS A FUCKING SHITHEAD WHO COULDN'T KEEP IT in his pants. I don't mean to offend the fine ladies reading my little book, but my dad went after skirts, and I'm being kind. "Skirt" means to get "go around" or outer parts, fringes. By either definition, my dad did it. I can offer evidence of that, but I respect the memory of my mom too much to make it public. I think he was a self-centered jerk, and while I'm a chip off that self-centered block, I've always been faithful to my wife.

My dad ran out before I could develop memories of him, but I've heard plenty of stories. Based on those stories and vague snapshots in my brain, I think he was an alcoholic. I'm told my mom and dad met as kids. My dad was in the military, as most men were in the '40s. His big feet saved his life. He got into the wrong boots and missed the flight to the war zone, where his entire squad died. God has a sense of humor.

I don't remember much about living with him. I know we once drove to Seattle to see my Aunt Helen, who may have been my dad's aunt. The road up there was slick with black ice. At one point, the car started to slide, and for the first time in my life, I saw genuine fear on my dad's face. To a little kid, your dad is supposed to be ten feet tall and bulletproof. Seeing him grip the steering wheel, his knuckles white, his eyes wide with panic, was more unsettling to me than the ice itself. It shatters the illusion that adults have everything under control. But we safely made it, and it was lovely at Aunt Helen's place on a quiet street on the city's west side. Her birthday was on New Year's Day, or close to it, and she was delighted with our surprise visit. For years afterward, my brother and I would laugh about how we rolled down a hill near her house, which was covered with pristine snow that January. Living in SoCal, we didn't know what to make of it, so like any kid, we made a snowman. I think it was the only snowman I ever made. It was so cold, we couldn't feel our hands, but we were having too much fun to care. Mom and Aunt Helen praised our snowman efforts, but I can't remember Dad saying anything. I remember wrestling with him in bed at our home in North Hollywood, which was fun, but I only have snapshots in my head—nothing but giggling here and there.

When I was five, maybe six years old, our family planned a trip to the San Diego Zoo and SeaWorld. To make it special, my brother and I were allowed to sleep in the living room the night before. What a treat! The adults partied in that room, which was much prettier than our bedroom. It felt like a real adventure.

Slivers of light crept under the full-length curtains, but otherwise it was pitch-black.

A loud pounding on our front door snapped us awake. The banging was so strong, the house began to shake. Mom came out of their bedroom and told us to go back to sleep. She said everything would be okay. Then she yelled at the thing hitting the door, "Go away! George isn't here!" George was our dad, and I could see his dark outline lying motionless in bed. My brother tried to get up, but Mom told him to stay put. The look in her eye said that going against her would mean terrible trouble for the two of us.

Just as quickly as it started, the pounding stopped, but seconds later, we heard what sounded like a wounded animal on the other side of our front door. I was sure we were going to be eaten by werewolves. I looked at my brother for answers, but it was so dark, I couldn't see his expression. I was terrified, sure we were going to be attacked. My mom pounded the door and, in a voice I'd never heard from her before or after, yelled, "Go away! Get out of here! Leave my family alone! I don't know where George is!"

I wondered what that wild animal wanted with my dad. Pride welled in my chest. I thought the thing would never get inside because Mom would protect us with her life. The unearthly sound became a human whimper, more pathetic than frightening. Years later, my older cousin told me that the "monster" was a person yelling in French. To an eight-year-old kid, it sounded like gibberish. She was pounding on our door, looking for my father to get money so she could get an abortion for the baby she'd conceived with him. He was such a coward; he sent five-foot-four-inch Mom to fight her off.

I'm so lucky he left us early in my life. He fathered two little girls with that woman and left them two-thirds of my brother's share of the estate when he died, even though we only met the girls one time in our entire lives.

When George was dying, we went to see him in Seattle so he could meet my son, his only grandson. I thought it was a dumb idea, but Mom, my brother, my son, and I enjoyed a nice drive, and it was fun to hear my mom reminisce about the good times she and my dad had. As long as she maintained her status as the firstborn's wife at family gatherings, she was able to forgive him for running around.

George had an old motorhome there, a dump that looked like it hadn't been touched in decades. How ironic for a car salesman to die in a mobile home. The kitchen was a mess—dirty dishes, trash everywhere. Every room in the place stank of animals, dirt, booze, cigarettes, and death. That sounds harsh, but the point of this story is that anyone can be down and out.

We hadn't seen dear old dad in years, but during that visit, he asked my brother and me—now in our early twenties—to wait in the kitchen. We obliged, thinking he wanted to apologize to Mom for the crap he'd put her through. We waited at the rusty, smelly table with our father's wife—or girlfriend—until Mom came out looking upset. When we jumped up and asked her what had happened, she insisted everything was fine and that she was ready to go whenever we were. Neither my brother nor I wanted to spend another minute in that sad trailer park.

We sped away, but a few miles down the road, she told us that he'd made a pass at her.

That frail, drooling man, riddled with cancer, his sons and his current wife on the other side of paper-thin walls, had asked my mom for a blowjob as a final favor. If she'd told us while we were still in the trailer, my brother and I would have been convicted of murder. My brother instinctively turned the car around, ready to go back and kick the shit out of him, but Mom stopped him. "What kind of example would that be for your nephew?" she asked. We drove home in disbelief.

Both Missy and I love my cousin Lynda, who has a great heart and stayed in touch with my father's family, which held yearly reunions at my uncle's house in Riverside, California. About twenty years after my dad died, I thought it might be nice to check it out and see the cousins after all that time. To say that Riverside is hot in the summer is like saying the Grand Canyon is a hole in the ground. It was 111 degrees, not a cloud in the sky, and it hadn't rained since before Christmas. No matter how high we cranked the air conditioner, we felt hot and dry. I was glad my sunglasses were super dark because the sun reflected off cars, pavements, and buildings, making it blinding even in the shade.

We drove down a dusty road to my uncle's house and parked in what I can only describe as a dirt lot. We were dying of thirst, dirty, and smelled like a two-hour ride in the sun. I'd warned Missy she might hear some off-color things about my parents. I gave her one last warning before we got out of the car. We found water, I found beer, and we were good to go.

As we unfolded our chairs, a man approached us. He was small in stature, maybe five feet two, appeared to be well into his eighties, and hadn't shaved for a while. He was clean but sloppy —old shoes, jeans, flannel shirt. "I'm so-and-so," he said. "You probably don't remember me, but your dad and I used to hang out. I loved that guy. He could really pick up the chicks. Must've fucked dozens, maybe a hundred, and that was while he was married".

I saw the disbelief on my wife's face. The first guy we met at our first family reunion in twenty-plus years was boasting about how my dad slept around on my mom.

The Choir Director

I had no male role models worth a damn until third grade, when at the age of nine, I met a man who would change my life forever. Frank St. Dennis, the director of our men and boys' choir, set me on a path of service, spirituality, kindness, love, and leadership.

Frank had a demanding day job and was very successful. Until I became a working adult, struggling to make ends meet, I didn't realize how much he sacrificed for the men, and especially the boys in his choir. Every Saturday during the school year, Frank taught us to sing. I'm a little tone-deaf, so I never really learned, but that didn't matter to Frank. He just wanted us to sing our hearts out. There were no auditions. If you wanted to be in the choir, you were in.

When I met him, Frank was likely in his late thirties and already sporting a bit of a pot belly, probably the result of corporate dinners and booze. Much later in life, I heard rumors that Frank was an alcoholic just like me. But as a kid, I never saw him do anything that resembled drunk behavior. He made sure his personal struggles didn't touch the church or the boys in the choir.

Frank made learning fun. The year before I joined the choir, he was still running relay races in the hall where we rehearsed, but some doofus fell into a pile of chairs and broke his arm in three places. We practiced in a high-ceilinged, plain space. The stage at one end, which had once been an altar, had working curtains and an ample backstage. You could tell it had once been a church, and the choir loft remained intact.

Frank understood the power of competition. He knew that win or lose, it brought us closer and made us a better choir. He also knew when to follow the rules and when to rebel. Without an instruction manual for running a boys' choir, he relied on instinct and came up with an ingenious game that didn't require running, hitting, or even standing. The game was called *You Bet Your Life Savers*. I don't remember all the rules, but the more lyrics you knew, the more candy you earned. We memorized every song, not because we had to, but because we *wanted* to. Somehow, this guy got us to do what teachers and parents couldn't. He made us use our little brains and work overtime for a reward.

Frank understood priorities. He recognized that some moments in life are bigger than the everyday. We'd meet at ten in the morning to warm up before Mass at 10:45. One morning wasn't about warm-ups; it was about history. The U.S. hockey team was playing the Russians, and Frank set up a TV so we could watch. This was before flat screens, when television sets were big, heavy machines with tubes that could implode when bumped. Moving one into a church hall on a Sunday was a bold move. I have no idea where he got it, but he made it happen. He understood what that game meant to us, and that day, we sang our little hearts out. More than forty years later, I'm still grateful for that day. It reminds me that I'm proud and lucky to be an American citizen, and reinforces the notion that a great leader understands priorities and the importance of moments.

Frank was kind—except when he wasn't. At the time, coaches could grab a kid by the collar and scare him into obedience. Frank was physical but never cruel. His signature move was pinching a kid's pinky flat into his palm—a two-second takedown that had the kid on his knees before he knew what hit him. It was like taking an uppercut from Mike Tyson. I'd see it coming, but I couldn't stop it. Eventually, I learned to pay attention the second Frank moved an arm.

But he was one of the kindest, most selfless people I've ever known. Every Christmas, we'd sing at nursing homes. On those trips, Frank was always our leader. He was a gentleman to the staff and kind to the patients. No matter how much he had to juggle, he never shortchanged anyone who needed to speak with him. Lessons learned: kindness and patience. The kindness stuck. I'm still working on the patience.

Frank knew how to be a good sport. He'd throw choir picnics and bring water balloons, fully aware that he'd get bombarded. And he took it like a champ. Lesson learned: a little self-deprecation keeps us humble.

One of my favorite Frank moments took place during a high-holiday rehearsal. Our church often hosted visiting priests —sometimes up to seventy-five of them—so there was a lot of politics behind the scenes, though I never quite understood it. One year, the bishop—maybe the archbishop—was coming to say Mass. Frank was stressed. In the middle of rehearsal, an altar boy delivered a message, and Frank stopped everything. In a loud, exasperated voice, he said, "You're taking my best choir boy away to carry some guy's white, pointy hat?" It was his way of telling us we'd be fine, even without our strongest voice. But it was also a nod of respect to the kid chosen to carry His Holiness's miter. We had a good laugh at Frank's borderline disrespect, then got back to rehearsal.

Frank also brought handbells to our church. As the story goes, he was at a choir director's conference, which sounds about as fun as a trip to the dentist. One evening as the sun was setting, he heard long, echoing notes that seemed to flow past him and continue on an invisible journey. As the sound grew closer, he noticed that the higher, more delicate notes wove through the sustained tones but were controlled and precise. Against the last rays of daylight, he saw a procession of bell ringers, their arms curling in perfect circular motions, their bells dancing with the music. It took his breath away. He stood there, tears in his eyes, completely captivated. At that moment, he decided our church needed handbells, and he committed to making it happen.

Handbells aren't a standard part of Catholic ministry, but Frank didn't care. When he asked our pastor for bells, a resounding "no" echoed through the land, but Frank wasn't one to let a good idea die. He started a fund. Donors could buy a bell in memory of a loved one with their name engraved on a plaque. He raised enough for four octaves of bells, and the bell choir was born. Decades later, those same bells were played at my brother's memorial.

Frank's example taught me leadership. His love taught me friendship. And his spirituality taught me grace.

I only made him really mad at me once, but it was bad. At bell choir rehearsal, I got talking with his son, Scott, and somewhere along the way, the conversation took a wrong turn. Scott was twenty-one and had been driving his souped-up Mustang for years, so he knew how to handle a car. On a break, we somehow got the idea to take his dad's company car for a quick ride around the block. I was fifteen or sixteen at the time, and thought it would be funny, although I don't think I had a driver's license yet. We found Frank's keys and took off. The car was exactly what I'd expect from Frank—clean, orderly, not a speck of dust. It was a Ford Gran Torino, boring but well-kept.

Meanwhile, back in the choir room, Frank spent the break completely unaware of our little adventure. When rehearsal was about to start again, he realized what we'd done. When Scott and I returned, the room was dead silent. Everyone was at attention behind their bells, so rigid the world might have been ending. After realizing we'd taken his car, Frank had gone back into the small choir room and emerged looking like an enraged

Native American Chief. His face was red, his breath was heavy, and smoke seemed to pour from his mouth and ears. If I hadn't been terrified, I might have laughed.

In a barely controlled voice, he said, "Go home. Rehearsal is over". Shivers ran down my spine. I'd never seen him like that. He told me, "Bill, I'll talk to you later". Then he turned to Scott. "Don't move." Scott didn't dare. No one did. Silently, the bells, tables, and equipment were put away. It was eerie. Then, in a voice filled with more disappointment than rage, he asked his son, "What were you thinking? You're supposed to be a leader here. That's a company car. What would have happened if there'd been an accident? I am so disappointed in you".

I felt he was saying that to me, too, and it was awful. Scott was in so much trouble, and I'd let Frank down. The next week, Scott told me they'd driven home in silence. I never heard more about it. Life went on, but the experience kept me on the straight and narrow for a long time.

Most boys left the choir at thirteen and didn't return to join the men's choir until they were much older. But my friend Tim, my brother Dennis, and I formed a new wave of younger singers who joined the old guard. I think some of the older guys were annoyed because rehearsals were no longer an excuse for a drinking party, but the camaraderie was great, and we had fun. The men's choir rehearsed on Thursday nights, and the guys went out afterward. The younger ones would head to Naugles, a burger joint started by a member of the Denny's family that sat about fifty people and had a drive-through. They served burritos and fries, and put shredded lettuce on their burgers. My brother always ordered a Macho Combo Burrito, which was stuffed with meat and beans plus all the fixings. At the time, it was the most food you could get in a single item.

The interior looked like the Partridge Family owned it, with a 1970s color scheme—avocado green with orange curtains on tinted windows. The burger and burrito wrappers were the same colors as the curtains and walls. The temperature was always a few degrees hotter than it needed to be, which allowed guys and girls to show off their midriffs and biceps. Attractive kids were always hanging around.

For the first twenty-plus years that Frank led the choir, he didn't use a baton. He used his hands, and it was beautiful to watch. At Midnight Mass in a dark church, standing in the loft with the light behind him, his silhouette cast giant, claw-like shadows that danced over the mosaic of Christ's walk to Golgotha on the walls, with a massive crucifix on the center altar at the apex. It was mesmerizing.

But at some point, Frank brought in brass and string instruments to accompany us, and suddenly, he had a baton. We all hated it and decided to do something about it. The choir always performed a few songs at Halloween events, making it the perfect setting for me to break that baton. And to really rub it in, I devised another prank.

A year before, Frank had been a contestant on the TV game show *Name That Tune*, hoping to win money for a new choir room. He crushed the competition until the final round, when he had to guess seven songs in thirty seconds. He nailed the first six in just ten seconds. Then, disaster struck. When the final song started playing, Frank froze. Ten seconds passed. Nothing. The host urged him to answer. Silence. Then, he began quietly singing the lyrics. The audience got restless. Five seconds left. Still nothing. The music reached the chorus, and… buzzer. Time was up. Just as the buzzer sounded, Frank muttered, "Leaving on a Jet Plane". He'd lost our new choir room by failing to guess the name of a massive hit song.

So, on the night of the Halloween party, I dressed as an airplane serviceman. When Frank saw me, he smiled. We had a live band, and I asked them to play "Leaving on a Jet Plane". The audience roared in the way you laugh when you're poking fun at a leader—half joyful, half nervous. I paraded through the crowd in a homemade cardboard airplane and circled Frank. He laughed at first, then his face started turning red. His look said *okay, funny, now stop*. But I didn't. I kept going until the song was over.

Frank took the stage, raised his baton, and tapped it on the stand. That was my cue. I got up, grabbed the baton, wrapped it on the stand, and—*snap*. The room exploded. Half the crowd gasped in horror. The other half howled with laughter. Frank walked toward me. My stomach tightened. Was I about to get the infamous pinky move?. Instead, he hugged my head like a father scolding a mischievous son. Then, he calmly walked back to the stand, reached into his sleeve, and pulled out another baton. Without missing a beat, he carried on like nothing had happened. Had someone tipped him off? Or was he just that prepared? With Frank, anything was possible.

I'm really conflicted about this next part. One side of me

says it's not important, it's nobody's business, and it had zero effect on my relationship with Frank or how any of us saw him. On the other hand, it gives me a chance to shed light on a group in our society that still gets the short end of the stick far too often.

Frank was gay.

You wouldn't know unless you knew him well. It wasn't something he advertised. But as I got older, I had the privilege of spending time with Frank outside of choir. From what I could see over the fifty years I knew him, he was in a loving, monogamous relationship with another man—someone I also became close with. I mention this not for gossip or shock value, but to offer a little understanding. The purpose of this book is to shine light where I can. I share the personal side of Frank's life as a message to anyone who fears gay people, to the bigots who judge lifestyles, and to those who hide behind religion—some of whom twist God's words into weapons of hate instead of love.

A wise friend once told me something like: "I don't care what you believe, but if your God isn't speaking with love, you've got the wrong God". Humans love whom they love. Just because someone loves a person of the same sex doesn't mean you should fear them, stop loving them, or distrust them around children. Frank was a gentle, kind, giving man who helped shape hundreds of young lives, including mine. Be open to those you don't understand. We're all children of God.

At the age of thirteen, Catholic kids go through the sacrament of confirmation. I was told that baptism meant my parents had declared I was a Catholic, while confirmation meant I'd chosen the religion for myself. I guess at a time when people died much younger, it made sense to consider that at thirteen, a kid has reached maturity. As part of that commitment, you choose a sponsor to guide you spiritually, like a godparent; you pick yourself. Family politics often play a role, but my mom told me I could ask anyone I liked.

The only man I wanted to ask was Frank. I joked with the other boys that from now on, he'd be known as Uncle Frankie. To this day, the name still sticks. My mom agreed he was a great choice but pointed out that, as far as we knew, he hadn't sponsored any of the other boys, and gently braced me for disappointment.

One day, after rehearsal, as we were cleaning up the hall, I got the courage to ask. "Mr. St. Denis, can I talk to you for a second?" He gave me his full attention. Even as a kid, I could feel how important that was. Later, I'd learn the word for it: *illumination*. To light someone up. To truly see and know them.

I took a breath. "As you know, I'm getting confirmed soon. I was hoping that you would be my sponsor. I'll understand if you can't". He looked thoughtful. I was sure he was searching for gentle words to let me down. Then he smiled big and said, "I would be honored". I held out my hand to shake his, trying to look cool, but he pulled me into a big bear hug. What a moment!. I'd asked the man I admired most, and he'd said yes. This was the male role model I'd longed for. A huge upgrade from my absent, fleabag dad. Frank was the real deal. A true godfather. A light.

Years passed, and Frank eventually moved to Morro Bay, a

quiet fishing town about five hours up the coast. We stayed in touch as best we could, but life moved on as it does. When my brother passed away, I hadn't seen Uncle Frank in a long time. We were planning a memorial, and I felt I should invite him. So many men whose lives Frank had touched would be there, and we were reuniting to play handbells, which we'd learned under his guidance. I called him, not sure what to expect.

He and his partner were kind, gentle, and loving. They were truly sorry to hear about my brother, but Frank's health had declined. He'd had a few falls. They were living in Palm Springs by then, and the drive would be too long, the emotions of the day too much. When we said goodbye, I felt sad and wished I'd done more to stay in touch. A little while later, the phone rang. It was Frank. He said, "We can't miss it. We'll be there".

What a gift. What a blessing. For me, for my brother, for so many of us. When Frank walked into that celebration, every parent, every choir boy, every friend was brought to tears. His warmth was still there. That old face still lit up the room. And for one last time, we were all together, bound by this remarkable man.

Frank passed not long after. I knew it was coming, but I still cried. Without him, there would have been no me. When we gathered to share stories, we realized how many lives he'd touched. His memorial service was bittersweet. I saw people I hadn't seen in decades, but it felt like yesterday because Frank had bound us all with his life, his love, and his ability to bring out the best in us. His son's eulogy said it best: "There is only one Frank St. Denis". And thank God, I knew him.

THE FATHERS I INHERITED

DENNIS, MY STEPFATHER-IN-LAW

I WISH I COULD HANG OUT WITH ROCKY BALBOA, CAPTAIN America, the Superman of *Truth, Justice, and the American Way* —not that Hero of the World PC crap DC Comics turned him into—Admiral James T. Kirk, and to a lesser degree, the Disney heroes: Moana, Simba, Jiminy Cricket, and Belle. It would be cool to hang around with Sylvester Stallone, Will Smith (minus the slap), the Rock, Tom Arnold, Kevin Costner, John Travolta, Adam Lambert, and Harry Chapin. I'd like to meet any pope, George Washington, or Ronald Reagan.

Maybe I'll meet them someday. But let me start with a great man I actually know: my wife's stepfather, Dennis. He is a kind and thoughtful man, full of wisdom and experience.

When we first met, I was already seriously dating his stepdaughter, and a total stranger in her tightly woven family. Dennis doesn't say much, but what he says is always worth hearing. He loved Missy's mom, Peggy, and her two daughters so much; I could see it in his eyes and his actions. He likes a sense of order about things. I'm not sure if that's the result of a strict childhood upbringing, a learned trait, or military training.

He taught me that unconditional love has conditions. You never got a free pass with him. He told me how he saw things, and if I didn't agree—fine. Not a lot of discussion. Missy and I used to hang out a lot with Dennis, Peggy, and another couple who were dear, longtime friends of Dennis's. One night, we were all at dinner, and the drinks were flowing. Out of nowhere, Dennis's friend said something insulting that deeply hurt Peggy. Dennis dropped the guy like a hot potato. Just like that, years of friendship were over. Nobody hurt his love. In that instant, he taught me exactly what it means to respect and protect your spouse.

When Missy and I got married, Dennis and Peggy had to work on the wedding finances. Dennis was a gentleman, always there to support us without creating difficulties. He taught me to let my spouse have her way. He always made his wife feel loved and supported. He showed me there's no place for ego in a happy marriage—not that I should let my wife walk over me, but that I should listen and agree with her. After my wife's mother passed away, Dennis remarried. His new wife, Pam, is lucky that he still works hard to be a good, fair husband. She's a loving woman who cares deeply for her family, which now includes Dennis's family. It's a beautiful union.

Dennis likes to keep things tidy, but once a year, his house becomes a pasta factory. Before Thanksgiving, all the women met to make a year's supply of ravioli, which they froze in shirt boxes from the dry cleaner. We'd eat them all year, and cook the last of the batch the following Christmas. While the women cooked, Dennis and I played golf. When we got back to the house, there was flour everywhere—on the floors, the counters, and floury handprints on the refrigerator. You'd think you were in a haunted house, like in those mystery movies where they blow the dust off a table to find the hidden clue.

The first time I witnessed this family tradition, Missy and Peggy were the only women in the kitchen, and they'd planned to make fifty boxes. When Dennis and I got back from golf, we asked how many they'd made. We'd been gone for five hours, so they had to be close to finished. I think the answer was twenty. Dennis heaved the sigh I've come to know and love, his way of saying, "Well, ain't this some shit. Let's start cleaning up". Over the years, Missy became a much better helper. Now, by the time we get back from golfing, the women are cleaning up. The ravioli tradition has been embraced by Dennis's wife, Pam, and he still cleans up.

One year, we had seven ravioli makers—Peggy, Missy, her sister Lisa, Lisa's daughters Sydney and Julie, Kathy, and Becca, who was out from Texas. When Dennis and I got back, the ravioli boxes were filled, and cleanup had started. Dennis looked around with a huge smile as Christmas music played, and he cracked open a beer. He thought it was sweet, but he cleaned up again. Christmas music was part of the tradition. Missy and Lisa hated that the Christmas season started too soon, so they agreed that we'd have no Christmas music until after Thanksgiving. Ravioli day was the exception.

Lessons from Dennis:

- Keep busy. He was always doing something—building, cleaning, refinishing. He never stood still.
- First things first. One weekend, my son and his girlfriend started making breakfast before doing the previous night's dishes. With his classic smile, Dennis said, "Let's get the dishes done before we make more dirty ones".
- Love your kids.
- Don't speak ill of anyone—even your enemies.
- Enjoy golf.
- Family is important. His interactions with his family helped me rejoin my own.
- The world doesn't revolve around you—a lesson I learned on the golf course.

That last lesson came on a chilly winter day. The sun was a medium orange rather than yellow, bright but a little overcast. A cool breeze ran through the course in the foothills of Castro Valley, Northern California. The ground was soft with scattered mud holes. Though it wasn't raining, there was moisture in the air, and the ball struggled to cut through the thick atmosphere. We shared the fairway with deer grazing on their morning meal. I don't know how they do it, but deer fill the air with silence the way a band fills it with music. The course was packed with beautiful, elegant creatures that bathed in the sunlight whenever it broke through the clouds and strutted around as if the golfers were just another element in their wide-open space.

At the time, I took the game very seriously. I was playing a couple of times a week, hitting the driving range just as often, and shooting in the nineties regularly. In my alcoholic mind, that was damn good, a classic redefinition of reality to fit my own perception. But that day, I played poorly, even for my sorry ass. Dennis' friend—we'll call him J—was having an incredible round. I was hating life on the course, and J was loving it. Dennis, ever even-keeled, enjoyed the game for what it was. Frustrated with my performance, I decided to grab a few beers at the turn.

For the record, this was twenty years before I admitted I was an alcoholic. If I'd been playing well, I'd have gotten a few to celebrate. With the beers in my hand and quickly getting to my head, my game only got worse, and I was getting mad. I abandoned golf etiquette, putted out of turn, cursed at every hole, and slammed my clubs into the ground. I even threw one in anger like a selfish child. J was playing the round of his life, but instead of letting him enjoy it, I brought him down. My bad attitude sucked the joy out of the day. When the round was over, I pouted off the course without saying a word.

Later that day, I realized Dennis was disappointed in me. Typical Dennis, he didn't say a word, just waited for me to come to my own realization. When I finally crawled out of my self-centered pride and apologized, he told me I needed to call J. So,

I did. I told him I had no right to take away his joy, that I had tried to make everyone around me as miserable as I was. I sucked. Dennis made me face it and learn from the experience. At the time, I didn't realize that what I was doing had a name. I was making amends.

In AA, Step Eight is making a list of all the people you need to apologize to. Step Nine is making amends. My sponsor says every "cringe-worthy moment" you can remember belongs on the list. One argument with Dennis made the cut.

It was the holiday season, and Missy and I were staying with Dennis and Peggy, as we always did. That evening, my brother and his girlfriend joined us for dinner. I don't remember what started the argument. Back then, when I fought, I had to win at any cost. My strategy was name-calling, bullying, and, in general, behaving like such an unbearable asshole that my opponent gave up. This was one of those fights. I got nasty. I called names. I threatened violence. It got so bad that Dennis or Peggy called my brother, who was halfway through his two-hour drive home, to come back and settle me down. That only made me angrier. By the time he arrived, law enforcement had been called. When the police showed up, I finally started to calm down.

It was one of the ugliest displays of behavior I can remember. There I was, surrounded by Christmas decorations, in a home filled with people I loved, screaming horrible things and threatening them. And yeah, I'd had way too much to drink. It wasn't the gin's fault. The fault was the asshole drinking the gin who didn't think alcohol was a problem.

The next morning, I didn't even want to crawl out of bed. Missy and I went to a movie so I wouldn't have to face Dennis and Peggy. But eventually, we had to go back. The air in the house was cold and flammable at the same time—like a gas grill with the propane left on, waiting for a match to set it off. For once in my life, I didn't strike the match. Instead, I turned off the gas.

Shockingly, I apologized. Even more shocking, they forgave me. And just like that, life went back to normal. Dennis would never have let me off the hook without an apology. He made sure I knew he was disappointed. But once I owned it, we could move forward. A few weeks later, I went to see Peggy alone. We talked, I apologized again, and by the end of the night, we were dancing together. That's when I knew we were okay.

Years later, when I worked Step Nine, that argument resurfaced. It was one of the most cringeworthy nights of my life. By then, Peggy had passed away, so my amends were a letter I read at her gravesite. As I headed back to the car, I saw a large gathering at another gravesite. A trumpeter began playing "Taps" as the sun set behind him, casting a golden glow across the sky. The melody echoed off the hillsides. For a moment, the world stopped to honor my mother-in-law. Thank you, God, for letting me know I was on the right track.

I still had to call Dennis. I had to relive my shame, own my role in it, and take responsibility—no excuses, no justifications. Just accountability. I told Dennis why I was calling. He paused and said he remembered the incident, now that I brought it up. Then he said, "All was forgiven years ago". The man who could rise above that kind of shit is the role model I thank God I've had for over twenty years.

ROSARIO PERRONE - MY FATHER-IN-LAW, RUSS

Russ is the only man I've called "Dad" since my father left. True moms and dads earn that title with patience, respect, kindness, caregiving, and love. Russ earned it one hundred-fold. He hated being called by his given name, Rosario, so he was Russ to everyone, but with me, he eventually responded to "Dad." He was an enigma, both loving and brutal. I've heard that he was tough on my wife and her sister while they were growing up. By the time I met him, he was more mellow, but he still could be frighteningly angry, foul-mouthed, and mean.

Russ and I freely teased each other. As I often tell my wife, boys tease to show love because we're too stupid to express it any other way. When I first met Russ, I was in my early thirties, and his daughter, Missy, was thirteen years younger, which he saw as a red flag. He put up with me, but I always had the feeling he wanted me to go away. He couldn't understand why I sold wine for a living and was constantly shocked at how well I was paid. He said he could tell the difference between a cheap wine and a good wine, but once it hit a certain level, he couldn't taste the difference. I'm not sure when he realized I wasn't going anywhere, but when he had to pay half the cost of a wedding for one hundred-plus guests at a fancy hotel, he came to grips with the idea. Years later, he told me the idea had bummed him out.

Russ was always good for a laugh. Sometimes he meant to

get the laugh, other times, he was embarrassingly funny. My sister-in-law and her family love to celebrate at a Benihana restaurant where the chefs cook at your table and make a show of slicing the meat. The table seats twelve, which makes it great for family gatherings. Once we could see that our chef was not Japanese but Hispanic. Russ asked him to make Japanese dishes and insisted on calling him "Jose," ignoring his name tag. It wasn't funny to watch Russ mock a well-trained professional chef, but the old man kept embarrassing himself, which made us laugh. When his daughters took him to the theater to see a musical, which was simultaneously translated into sign language, Russ loudly asked why a deaf person would go to a musical. He wasn't trying to be funny.

But he always meant well, and you couldn't find a better guest. He was gracious and kind to everyone, and, perhaps because he was in sales, he knew what it meant to be an entertainer. He was a great conversationalist and a great listener, asking questions about people's lives. It was a learning experience to watch him work a room.

We occasionally went out for Chinese food at a restaurant near our house, a typical place with a bar to the right and two dining rooms on the left with tables seating ten or twelve and a lazy Susan in the middle. Noise spilled from the kitchen, voices speaking—sometimes yelling—in Chinese, and pots and pans clattering. The menus were large, with many items, and a lot of the prices had been scratched out with new prices written in. Since Russ was paying, he usually did all the ordering. He always ordered pot stickers with vinegar and chili oil to start, then hot-and-sour soup or sizzling rice soup. Unlike most people, he'd eat his fill of one item at a time. The first time I took Missy out for Chinese food, I noticed that she ate it in a specific order—appetizers, then soup, then entrée. I told her dad that was odd, and he asked, "Where do you think she learned that?"

One night, Russ hosted a family dinner for fourteen people in a private room at a restaurant. We later dubbed it "the Pope's Room," because the centerpiece was a pope's head. The space needed to be upgraded. It was windowless, so we felt as though we were being locked in a dungeon, but the scent of garlic wafting from the kitchen helped mask the musty odor, and the hum of the bustling restaurant below created a Disneyland-like atmosphere—real, but not quite reality. The food was mediocre Italian, but it was festive, and at least none of us had to cook that night.

At the end of the meal, Russ got livid. His face turned bright red, and I could tell that he wanted to punch something. He stormed out, swearing, "Those bastards. They'll never see me again, and they won't get another dime of my money. No more parties here". Years later, I learned the cause of his outburst was that although we'd ordered desserts from the menu, we'd also brought a cake. It was a family tradition to celebrate with an ice cream cake from Baskin-Robbins. When we called ahead to explain this, the restaurant didn't mention that they charged $ 2.50 per person for cutting and serving the cake. They just added it to the bill, which drove Russ crazy. At the time, it freaked me out, but looking back, it's kind of funny.

Russ wasn't one to feel bad about his words or actions. He was like Popeye: "He is what he is". There was a time when AJ, my young nephew, was obsessed with action figures. I don't remember the brand, but it doesn't matter. Growing up, I had my own epic battles with GI Joes and Major Matt Mason dolls, so I could relate. AJ loved these toys and played with them all the time. One day, during a holiday, like Thanksgiving or Easter, Russ asked AJ to do a chore while he was playing with his figures. AJ didn't respond right away. Russ asked again. AJ said, "I'll do it later, I'm in the middle of something". And Russ lost it. He grabbed the toys, told AJ they were stupid, and made AJ feel like he was stupid for playing with them. Technically, Russ didn't call AJ stupid, but that's how AJ heard it. The kid froze, caught between wanting to scream and cry. Thankfully, he ran off before the situation escalated. A few hours later, Russ, genuinely remorseful, apologized to AJ. It was the first time I'd ever seen the man reflect on his actions in that way.

Russ was a tough guy, always ready to threaten physical violence if things got out of hand, which was funny, considering I was twenty years younger and had about a hundred pounds on him. He often told me stories about the fights he'd had with his brother—a product of his time and upbringing. I came to know him through holiday cigars and realized that the "tough guy" exterior was just that—an exterior. He was a loving father and grandfather. We talked about everything—sports, politics, family dynamics.

The worst part about Russ? He was a 49ers fan, which made sense since he'd lived in the Bay Area for so long. We argued nonstop about the Rams versus the 49ers. I didn't have much ground to stand on—the 49ers were a dynasty, and the Rams... We'd had one Super Bowl win, back when they were in St. Louis. Joe Montana was the GOAT in my eyes, and the 49ers had legendary players like Ronnie Lott and Jerry Rice. I managed to get season tickets to a Rams game and took Russ to see the 49ers. It rained, of course. Every time I went to a game against the 49ers, the weather seemed to turn sour. The stadium was packed, mostly with 49ers fans. The LA Coliseum is a dump built decades ago, and we were stuck in the rain with no cover, no shade, and hard, uncomfortable seats.

You haven't lived until you've peed in a trough shoulder to shoulder with another guy. I never want to use a communal pee trough again. The bathrooms smelled like the piss had seeped into the walls. I think that year it rained two days in So Cal, and one was when we went to the game. It was a California rain. What other states call drizzle, we call rain. Just damp enough to make the concrete beast smell like the dinosaur it was. Since it was raining, we took umbrellas, but we didn't know we'd have to check them at the gate. By the time we reached our seats, it was pouring. I asked Russ if he really wanted to be there, and the look on his face said, "Get me the hell out of here!" It hit me then that he wasn't there for the game. He was there to spend time with me. That made my day. We left early, and for months, Russ complained about leaving his umbrella behind. That Christmas, I wrapped up an umbrella I bought at Walmart. He appreciated the joke.

In all the time I knew him, I only lost my temper with Russ

once. Needless to say, I'd been drinking. He'd just returned from a trip to the Grand Tetons and was talking about how breathtaking and life-changing the experience had been. I said I couldn't care less about mountains or trees, or whatever the Grand Tetons were. He kept insisting that I was wrong and had to go there. I'd rather go to the dentist. I thought the Grand Tetons had been a honeymoon destination forty years before, a favorite of couples who couldn't afford anything else. I told him I wasn't interested. He couldn't believe it. He'd found something life-changing, and he wanted to share it. As he got more animated about how amazing it was, I became more animated about what a waste of time it would be. I told him he couldn't force me to like mountains. We agreed to disagree, but we were just short of screaming at each other. The next morning, I apologized for treating him poorly, and he shrugged it off like it was no big deal. To him, it really wasn't. He'd grown up with loud conversations and could let an argument roll off his back like a good morning hug.

I loved that man, and we had deep, meaningful conversations. He wanted nothing but the best for his daughters, and his grandchildren were his treasures. He'd grown up at a time when men didn't show much emotion, but he was full of love and kindness. He always did the right thing, and his family always came first. It's easy to poke fun at him, but probably more than anyone else, he showed me what it meant to be a good, strong, loving man.

Thanksgiving was Russ's favorite holiday. He loved everything about it—the meal, the family unity, the secular aspects, football, and most of all, the traditions. For us, the holiday started on Tuesday and didn't end until Sunday, sometimes Monday. Russ would show up on Tuesday with groceries for Wednesday's dinner. He'd bring his own eggs, butter, bread, and cranberries. He only occasionally used what we had on hand. He even brought his own orange juice and vodka for Ramos Fizzes. He really wanted to host the holiday, but since the rest of the family lived in SoCal, we held it at our house.

He'd drive from Arizona in his sleek, black sports sedan, usually arriving in slightly ratty sweats. He'd hit the bathroom, then unpack everything he'd brought in a deep-red cooler. Missy and I still use that cooler, although the zipper sticks like crazy. With that out of the way, he'd look at me and say, "Yes, I'd love one". I'd ask, "Neat or rocks?" We have a beautiful dark Ethan Allan dining table, and we hated that Russ scattered his groceries all over it, so after a few years, we set up tables in the garage to hold the ingredients and serving dishes. Russ would stand at his favorite spot near the fridge in our kitchen, double and triple-checking his list. When it was all set, we'd sit down for another cocktail and catch up on the news in our lives. Russ stayed at Missy's sister's place because he loved being around his grandkids, so, after that, he left.

The day before Thanksgiving was quiet until Russ showed up with the kids. He'd reread his recipes and begin chopping onions, celery, and bread for the stuffing. At some point, we'd order dinner—either pizza or Italian takeout, which we'd eat on the kitchen table because we'd already started setting the dining room table for the next day's feast. My niece, Sydney, made place cards so everyone knew where to sit. Russ wasn't content until everything that could be prepped for the next day was done. Then we enjoyed a scotch. He didn't show his happiness much, but I could tell how proud he was of his daughters and grandkids.

Russ and the grandkids spent the night before Thanksgiving at our house so he could start early the next day. He was always the first up and made us a breakfast of Swedish pancakes—a tradition Missy and her sister loved. The first Thanksgiving after Russ passed away, my nephew AJ wanted to make Swedish pancakes. He knew it was important to his mom and the rest of the family. That year, the pancakes were a little thicker, but they were made with love. After the pancakes, it was Ramos Fizzes and dinner prep. Russ made stuffing, gravy, cranberries with oranges, and cornbread, and he carved the turkey. As we brought the dishes to the table, he'd photograph or videotape the holiday, making sure to get everyone in the shots. Then, we'd eat at our crowded table. After dinner, we'd enjoy spirits and conversation. The next day, we'd do it again with friends, sometimes as many as fifty people. Russ told me he didn't like the day after Thanksgiving anymore—too many people, too much going on. He cherished the time with his daughters and grandchildren and made Thanksgiving special for all of us.

One year, Russ, his ex-wife (Missy's mom), her husband Dennis, and Russ's long-time companion Theresa were at dinner, and they all got along. I realized why Missy had grown up to be such a graceful and loving person. She'd had her share of drama, but the core of her family had always shown respect and a genuine support for one another.

When my wife's sister Lisa was getting married, Russ had lost a lot of weight and was beginning to look sickly. I asked him about it, and he told me he had some medical issues but didn't want to go into details. I figured it was cancer. He swore me to secrecy. It was his way of protecting everyone so they wouldn't worry. He told his girls he was fine. He'd always taken care of them and didn't want them to know how sick he was. He stubbornly believed he would beat it and be fine.

And he did. He got better, and we were blessed with many more years with him before his health finally failed again.

When the end finally came, he was still trying to hide it to protect his girls. Finally, against his wishes, his companion, Theresa, called to let them know he was in the hospital. Missy and I dropped everything and drove to Arizona. When he'd felt unwell, he'd gone to see his doctor, who immediately sent him to the ER. He never came home.

When we arrived at his hospital room, he was sitting up, working on his computer. I believe he didn't want us to know how sick he really was. The Covid pandemic had just begun, and I had to drive home for a few days. When I called Missy to tell her I was on my way back, she said, "Don't bother". I asked if he was gone, and she sobbed, "Yes".

Sadly, due to Covid, we couldn't have a proper service for Russ. Part of me thinks he would have preferred it that way—no fuss, no big gathering, just his memory carried on by those who loved him. He left a legacy of love behind. He was a tough man with old-fashioned ideas who had a rough exterior. I believe that when he passed, his biggest sorrow was not being able to see his grandchildren grow up, and they'll never forget him. AJ is driving now, and he often thinks about his grandpa behind the wheel. I don't think a day goes by that Sydney doesn't miss him deeply. I don't talk to Lisa much about him. Missy is still in shock. He was supposed to live forever. She's very much aware that he helped her become the woman she is today. Her grit and power come from him. She takes no bullshit from anyone, as he showed her through example.

Some evenings when we're watching TV, out of the blue, she'll say, "I miss my dad," and it breaks my heart. I feel the loss for all of us who loved him. He wasn't perfect, none of us are, but he was a loving dad, a good friend, and a great man. If I accomplish even a small percentage of what he did, mine will have been a life well lived. He once said that you can judge a man by his friends. I believe that, and I'm grateful that Russ and I were friends.

I know he's watching.

E-TICKET RIDE

Memorial Day, May 27, 2024, started out like any other Monday. My wife had the day off, so I was a little bummed that I had to go to an AA meeting that morning, but I was the secretary for that meeting and had to fulfill my commitment.

I arrived early, and one of the regulars showed up around the same time. His car was in the shop, so he'd ridden his bike over after going to the gym. I thought, *"What a commitment!"* He complained that he was hot and sweaty, and I could see that he was, although it was a bit chilly that morning. He grabbed the room key from its usual spot and unlocked the doors. I started the coffee, and he began setting up the books.

At that meeting, we placed a copy of the book *Daily Reflections* and a prayer book at the end of every row, and scattered a few extras on the other seats. We set up the literature stand on the back counter. The meeting had a hard plastic case with large slide buttons that locked and unlocked, where they kept all the literature, a large-print prayer book for whoever was reading that day, and a plain white two-inch binder for daily recap sheets and collections. As secretary, it was my responsibility to record visitors, newcomers, and the names of people who read aloud.

The third person to arrive was surprised that the meeting had already been set up, because he usually took care of that. He asked if the coffee was ready. "Of course," I replied, "first thing after turning on the lights". Delighted, he hurried to grab a cup. On Mondays, attendance at meetings is usually light, and since it was also a holiday, I expected a small crowd, so I'd only made one pot of coffee instead of the usual two. However, I'd prepped a second filter and pitcher of water in case, and as it turned out, I needed them. Eleven people showed up.

The meeting was uneventful, and I didn't share. As I was leaving, one of the long-time members mentioned that I was unusually quiet. "Nothing wrong," I said. "I'm fine, just a little tired".

Just a Quick Nap

I got home a little before nine that morning, and my wife was still asleep, wrapped in our blue sheets and white comforter. Our beagles, Joy and Lilo, were sleeping with her, so I decided to get some extra rest, too. Since I was only planning to nap briefly, I didn't bother to undress.

The next thing I remember, I was sitting on the toilet and

heard my wife enter the bedroom. "Hello?" I called. "Hello," she replied.

I woke up in an ambulance.

I'd passed out, and my poor wife had no idea why. She later told me that she asked if I could make it to the floor, and I responded, "Where is the floor?" She called 911, locked up the dogs, and opened the door for the paramedics.

The ambulance arrived in seconds. Thank God, a new fire station had been built around the corner from our house. Shortly after the ambulance arrived, neighbors came over to check on us, but I have no idea what they said. I was completely out of it.

The paramedics got me on a stretcher, down our double-wide staircase, and into the rig. Ironically, the staircase had been designed that way to make room for a wet bar. I must have been in and out of consciousness for about fifteen minutes.

When I finally started to come around, I felt like I was on an E-ticket ride at Disneyland — the best and scariest of the attractions.

The Matrix and the Paramedics

It felt like I was in the *Matrix*, fighting with people, convinced they were trying to kill me. I struggled to break free as they held me down. It was freezing, but I was sweating. The space around me was all white — no walls, no ceiling, just an endless sterile white. I could hear voices saying, "Sir, calm down." But I couldn't.

Somewhere in my struggle, I believed I'd punched somebody. Then I started to settle in and accept this new reality where there was no wife, no puppies, no liver cirrhosis.

I had a flash of a public street that looked like my old reality. I saw one of my neighbors walking home. And just like that, I was back, surrounded by five paramedics. They explained I had passed out due to low blood sugar, and they were taking me to the hospital.

My wife appeared in my field of vision. I could see she'd been crying, and her face was as pale as the walls in my hallucination. The sky above her was gray, but street signs and trees began to regain their color.

"Am I getting a new liver?" I asked. "Not right now," she answered. I knew the answer, but I needed to ask. "Am I really sick?" She assured me that I was. Reality fully returned.

The paramedics wheeled me into the ambulance, and I panicked again. "Are you taking me to Kaiser?" They were. "Kaiser La Palma?" Yes. I relaxed slightly.

One of the paramedics pointed at my jeans, which were still draped around my knees. Yep. I had definitely been in the bathroom. The paramedics were so nice, and I was afraid I'd punched one of them, but I later realized they were all in great shape, and if I'd hit one of them, my hand would have been bruised.

The Aftermath

The clouds seemed very low as they wheeled me into Kaiser. Everything around me looked grey, which was strange because I could see the sun trying to poke through. When I heard Missy's voice, I felt better. I wasn't sure what was happening, so I assumed it was connected to my liver issues, but the culprit was my blood sugar. If I'd had a protein bar at ten that morning as usual, the entire episode could have been avoided.

The emergency room staff had to deal with another bad sign: my temperature. I was sweating, and they didn't know if my body was fighting the cold or the physical exertion of battling imaginary demons. I was so cold that the nurse couldn't get a reading with her electronic thermometer. Next step was a rectal thermometer. They had to use it twice before I warmed up.

I was placed under a sheet with a warm air blower attached. It felt like a gentle, giant body hug. As I began to recover, my friends, Tim and Kay, showed up, and I so appreciated their love and support. Kay had made a quilt with Rams' fabric and put my name on it. I was finally warm and comfortable in so many ways.

I asked the nurse if I could eat, and they gave me the first of the three turkey sandwiches I had in the hospital — probably more sodium than I'd consumed in any three days over the prior eighteen months.

Missy had been perfect under pressure. Later that first morning, she'd called my Kaiser Permanente therapist and my

AA sponsor and texted everyone to update them on my condition. She is one of the bravest, smartest people I know. I'm so grateful that she'll be my primary caregiver when I have major surgery to replace my liver.

I spent the night at the hospital for observation and went home the next day with a little contraption to prick my finger so we could test my blood sugar. I'm writing this two days after the incident, and my blood sugar is within normal range. We hope this is the last surprise on the journey to a new liver and lifelong sobriety, but if it isn't, we'll take it one day at a time.

What Happens in Vegas

EVERY YEAR, *WINE SPECTATOR* MAGAZINE HOSTS A TOP 100 Wines event. You pay a lot of money to taste what they've deemed the top one hundred wines in the world that year.

Before I gave up drinking, two of my favorite things to say about wine were: "Relax, it's only rotten grape juice," and, when asked what my favorite was, I'd respond, "The one in my glass."

One year, I was invited to pour wine at the event for a winery my company represented. I was thrilled, but having tasted some of the most expensive wines on the planet, I'd concluded that the emperor was naked. Don't get me wrong, some wines are better than others, and some are truly great, but there's no divinity in wine production. The prices some "collectible" wines command are appalling.

The event was a two-night affair in Las Vegas. The halls looked like a typical trade show with rows of tables covered in black linen displaying bottles or crystal decanters. Tuxedoed servers slid through the crowd, white napkins hung over their forearms, keeping the area spotless. It looked like a cartoon classic ballroom—until decorum broke down, and the crowd began to push and shove for an ounce of precious liquid. They'd sniff, then taste, swirling it around in their mouths before spitting it into cups or spittoons.

Five minutes after the doors opened, all those pristine linen tablecloths were stained. The editor of the magazine was already drunk, sweaty, and chain-smoking cigars. Quite elegant!

THE GHOSTBAR INCIDENT

After the first night of tasting, my employer, the winery's representatives, and I went to dinner at Nobu, one of my favorite restaurants. It's part of a small but very exclusive chain, and even in Las Vegas, where the celebrity-chef experience is a bit cookie-cutter, the food is exceptional. There are other truly spectacular dining experiences in Las Vegas, like Joël Robuchon, Guy Savoy, and Bazaar Meat by José Andrés, that also come to mind. We ate, drank, and enjoyed sake in traditional wooden cups.

After dinner, we all went our separate ways. Some went to gamble, the smart ones to bed. I went off in search of more to drink with my supervisor, dragging my wife along.

We went up to the Ghostbar at the Palms Casino Resort, which was a happening place at the time with long curtains, plenty of couches, and several dance floors. When we arrived, it was maybe 10:30, early for the club scene. The dance floors were nineteen or twenty-nine floors above the ground and made of plexiglass, so you could see straight down under your feet.

My wife was drinking Cosmopolitans. I can't remember if I ordered a martini or scotch, but my boss ordered cognac. The server said I'd have to go to the bar to get that.

I told my wife and boss to hang tight and went to the bar, which was on one of the plexiglass floors. Although it was early, the line was long, so it took about twenty minutes before I got to the bartender, who then told me I'd have to go to a different bar for cognac. Annoyed, I took the drinks I had and delivered them to my wife and boss, then went to the next bar, where I was sent to yet *another* bar.

Now I was seriously pissed. My boss was waiting, my wife was trying to make small talk, and these assholes were sending me on wild goose chases.

A guy in a suit asked how I was enjoying the club.

I yelled, "This club is fucked up! I can't even—"

Before I could finish, a giant man lifted me from behind. I grabbed the bar for balance, and suddenly, two more guys in black suits appeared.

"What the fuck is happening?" I yelled.

They told me I was being evicted.

"All I want is a fucking cognac for my boss!"

The Haunted Mansion Elevator

Before I knew it, I was in an elevator, the giant let go, and I regained my balance. Two large men in suits stood in front of me, arms crossed, like a bad movie.

My left index finger was throbbing and gushing blood. I shook it off, and the giant said, "Don't do that. You might have AIDS and could kill me."

What a ridiculous comment! But it shook me to reality. I realized I was in an elevator moving quickly. No windows. It was like the Haunted Mansion at Disneyland, but terrifyingly real. They could kill me, and no one would know.

"My wife and boss are upstairs," I pleaded. "Can I get a message to them?"

"No, motherfucker."

When the elevator stopped, my wife and boss were waiting. They told me the club claimed I'd threatened an employee. I yelled at the security guys. "Fuck you! I was just trying to get a drink in your shitty place!"

My boss and wife calmed me down. I was still bleeding.

A cop showed up, heard my story, and said, "Sorry for the mistreatment. I'll call an ambulance." A few minutes later, he returned. "Sorry you had an accident, but there are no witnesses of wrongdoing. Have a good night."

And there it was—the truth of the marketing slogan "What happens in Vegas stays in Vegas."

Zero Tolerance & Stop the Bleeding

There we were in the parking lot of the Palms Casino Resort. My finger was still bleeding enough to remind me that the night had gone sideways. It was late, and I had a distributor meeting in the morning.

I half-expected we'd been kicked out of the hotel, but our room key still let us in. My wife did her best to wrap my finger, but between the pain, the humiliation, and the neon glow of Vegas streaming through the window, I couldn't sleep. At some point, I bled through the towels, so I asked Missy to call the front desk for more. They sent towels, bandages, and a generic apology. "Sorry about the club. The hotel and the club are run separately. We hope you enjoy the rest of your stay."

The next morning, our distributor, a Las Vegas local, collected my boss and me. In the car, I asked him why security had acted so aggressively, and he explained the club had a zero-tolerance policy. The moment I dropped an F-bomb at a manager, I was done. No questions. No exceptions.

"Seems extreme," I said.

"When you've got gangsters with guns frequenting the place, strict rules keep people alive."

Fair enough.

At the meeting, my finger started bleeding again, so when it was over, I found an urgent care clinic. The doctor took one look and said, "Nothing to stitch up. The skin's gone."

Until that moment, I wasn't entirely convinced the jolly giant in the black suit hadn't stabbed me. I had no idea how I'd gotten hurt, but then it clicked. When I was yanked off my feet and grabbed the bar for balance, I must have caught a finishing nail underneath, and it had torn a chunk of skin away.

The only option was cauterization. First, they numbed the

area, which burned like hell. Then the doctor sprinkled ignitor powder on the wound and said, "This is gonna hurt."

It did. Like, *super* hell.

But the worst of it was over fast, and the doctor gave me the classic "take two aspirin" advice. Please. This was Vegas. There was tequila everywhere. They wrapped my finger and told me to keep my hand elevated for the next day or risk having to redo the procedure. I'd rather lose the finger.

I still had another night of tasting, and Missy had noticed blood all over the back of my tuxedo jacket. The Palms didn't have same-day cleaning, so we had to take a taxi, drop it off, and pick it up two hours later—an emergency cleaning that cost over a hundred bucks.

That night in my freshly cleaned tux, I tried to enjoy the event despite my bandaged-up hand. People kept asking what had happened. They'd used so much gauze on my wound that my middle finger looked like a mini baseball bat.

And since I had to keep it raised, I spent the whole evening unintentionally flipping off the wine industry.

Cheers to that.

ACT III: THE WORK IN PROGRESS

Borrowed Voices, Shared Reflections

Well, you have read about Bill the asshole, the motherfucker, the king of all he could see. You have read about the people who helped shape me—some showing me exactly how to be, and others showing me exactly what *not* to be. You've been with me through near-death experiences, trips to the emergency room, and giants kicking my ass.

Now, we enter the final section of this book.

This section is about the man I am now—nowhere near perfect, struggling to even be good at times, but aware and humble. And I couldn't have become him—or continued to make changes—alone. We say in A.A. that it is a "We program, not a Me program," and I know that is true.

The first chapter of this final section is a few stories and writings that helped me make profound changes in my life. Yeah, that's right, the drunk egomaniac is giving up space to others. Before I got sober, my ego would have never let another voice into my book. I had to own it, control it. It had to be *mine*. Now, I know I have only what my Creator gives me, and the authors of these writings are absolute gifts. I am deeply grateful to share them with you.

I once heard Pat Monahan, the lead singer of Train, sing a great rendition of Journey's "Don't Stop Believin'". The crowd went crazy, and he said, "I wish I'd written that song. I've written a lot of songs, but I wish I'd written that one."

That's exactly how I feel about the stories I'm about to share with you.

They've moved me in different ways, and I'm so grateful the authors agreed to let me include them in this book.

The Bluebird

If you want to know what my ego cost me during my drinking years, this poem by Richard H. sums it up perfectly. For decades, I was so busy being the smartest guy in the room—so busy defining, judging, and controlling every little detail of my life—that I missed the actual miracle of living. I traded wonder for certainty, and I missed the bluebirds because I was too busy *"nodding like an expert."* Today, my sobriety requires me to practice forgetting what I think I know. Richard's words are a beautiful, humbling reminder of why I have to stay awake, stay present, and stop acting like I already have it all figured out.

The Bluebird

By Richard H.

I used to think the miracle was rare.
That it only showed up on special days,
    in special places, for special people.
Then one day, a bluebird crossed my
    path.
No announcement. No spotlight. Just
    wings and breath and now.
And for a moment, I was there.
No past. No future. No story.
Just seeing.
And that moment changed me.
Not because I found something…
But because I lost something.
I lost my innocence with wonder.
Because after that, I "knew."
I knew what a bluebird looked like. I
    knew where they lived. I knew what
    to expect.
So when the next one came…
I wasn't there.
I was thinking. Labeling. Comparing.
    Remembering.
"Oh yeah… that again."

And it flew right past my life while I
    nodded like an expert.
Aspiration says, "Get somewhere."
Inspiration says, "Be here."
Aspiration climbs. Inspiration listens.
Aspiration is hungry. Inspiration is
    awake.
And hunger never tastes the meal.
Presence does.
We don't miss miracles because they stop
    happening.
We miss them because we stop noticing.
We trade mystery for memory.
We trade wonder for certainty.
We trade now for "I already know."
But life never repeats itself.
Not this breath. Not this face. Not this
    sunrise. Not this conversation.
Not this moment.
Every bluebird is the first one—
If you're paying attention.
So now, I practice forgetting.
Forgetting what I think I know. Forget-
    ting who I think I am. Forgetting
    where I think I'm going.
So I can meet what's actually here.
Again. And again. And again.
Because the truth is—

I never stopped seeing bluebirds.

I just stopped seeing.

Until now.

The Unbearable Weight of My Carry-On Baggage

Sometimes someone else's story cracks something open in us. My friend Debbie wrote a powerful, four-part series for my *Sober Steps Journal*. Her journey is a mirror of what so many of us go through: the illusion of having it all together on the outside while unraveling on the inside. I have distilled her incredible, multi-page story down to just a few hundred words here, but even in this short form, the impact is undeniable.

By Debbie

For twenty-five years, my twenty-one-inch black Tumi carry-on suitcase went everywhere with me. Hawaii, Paris, Tokyo, you name it. My hand was always wrapped tightly around its handle, eagerly pulling it to the next professional adventure.

But the trip that stands out more than any other was on June 15, 2009. That was the day I boarded a plane to Minnesota with my Tumi bag, heading to the Hazelden Treatment Center.

My life had become unmanageable. I didn't drink in my younger years—having grown up with an alcoholic mother and a brother addicted to heroin—but life happened. A first marriage plagued by secrets and my ex-husband's addiction left me navigating life as a single, working mother raising my beautiful daughter. It was exhausting. I soon discovered that two or three glasses of wine before bed blotted out the stress, fear, and resentment completely. Problem solved, right? Wrong.

It took ten years of gentle prodding from a therapist to finally get me to a folding chair. I vividly remember my first A.A. meeting. I tucked myself into a corner, full of belligerent skepticism, critically sizing everyone up. I read Step One and thought, *I don't belong here. My circumstances just need some adjustments.* But then I watched people walk to the front, collect their sobriety chips, and say those three words. Whatever God existed in that room compelled me to stand up. Drenched in sweat and shaking with fear, I walked to the podium, took a chip, and said into the microphone: "My name is Debbie, and I am an alcoholic." That simple act of confession gave me my first glimmer of hope.

I realized that for years, I had used alcohol to avoid true connection. My disease made me isolate, rebuffing others to avoid real or imagined emotional loss. What I learned at Hazelden, and in the sixteen-plus years since I made that trip, is that my soul—untethered by fear— actually *craves* connection.

Today, my faithful Tumi bag still travels with me, but to much better places. Recently, after a Sunday brunch with friends, we met in the program and at a Lakers game. My husband and I drove to Capistrano Beach to housesit overlooking the Pacific. Tumi in tow, I watched a spectacular sunset I would have completely missed if I hadn't surrendered back in 2009.

We really are the lucky ones.

THE RELAPSE

I met a young woman in Day Treatment who could have been the poster child for innocence and courtesy. She was super shy, but as I got to know her, I realized that beneath her meek presentation, she had a great inner strength. I think she was a little shell-shocked from dealing with the trauma of losing her mom and her sister—who was also her best friend—to cancer within months of each other.

One day, she called and said she was done with AA.

I was worried, but my sponsor pointed out that she might be a "normie." Her trauma may have given her a reason to drink, but that reason ended when the trauma went away. Since she left AA, I haven't asked about her sobriety. It's her business, but if she ever wants to talk to me, she knows I'm here for her. If she can drink like a lady, our hats are off to her.

Before she left, she shared this poem at an AA meeting. It hit me so hard, I asked if I could use it.

November Second

By Sasha Albano

I drink two cups of mourning coffee
    with cream and conchas crumbly as
    my sticky heart cutting out my love
    for you at the Ofrenda wishing you
    were here to whisper your wonderful,
    wind-up words.

I walk from the library, and I watch the
    sky, the clouds that are you blushed
    pink, and I want to fly up and
    touch you

I drink the water of life, straight from
    the kitchen tap, warm and metallic
    watering something dark at the base
    of my spine something spindly and
    wicked, curled up away from the
    sun, and it sends me walking like a
    moth to string lights. I flutter, and it
    pulls me into its beating pulse,
    starry-eyed, I wonder

I have my first drink, tart and pink and
    pick-me-up warm in the corner bar
    watching people come and go,

relaxed, but for that small gnawing
ache those fingers that curl around
my ribs, and I chase after it, sip
by sip

I have my second drink, gold mapley
tequila I shiver and I eat away at a
sandwich wondering where you are
now, and if you see me, send me
some sign, I think, and the evening
light flashes in the windows

I have my third drink, I am with a friend
now, and I'm wind dark and giggly
all these humans pressed around me,
breathing, and I'm so happy to be
alive, so happy that I'm here, and I
never want this feeling to end

I have my fourth drink, my fifth, my
sixth. I drink half a bottle of banana-
flavored wine, and I watch the sunset
sway to music and feel something
slipping. I want to be where you are.
I want to be with you

And the feeling is sudden, overpowering,
the dark thing inside me unfurls,

takes my hand, and I'm walking
again

I have my seventh drink, my eighth, I
    start losing count, the universe is
    zoomed into this fire pit in front of
    me, and I can feel every molecule in
    my body vibrating. I sip as if from an
    infant's bottle, I watch the planes
    overhead, lined up like stars, and I
    swoon

The whole world spins, and it's getting
    darker. I can't feel you anywhere. I
    grasp for you desperately maybe I
    drink more. I don't remember

I remember moments of walking home,
    tripping over cracks in the sidewalk,
    and following the lampposts home I
    remember my key in the door. I
    don't remember making that phone
    call, but I remember wanting to fall
    asleep and dream an eternal dream.

There was a light on in the hallway, and I
    lay on the bathroom floor soaked
    with sweat and all alone my insides

poisoned, and the black thing inside
of me was on the ceiling watching

I wake with a terrible jolt in the morning, sicker than I've ever been. I can't
move but cry into my pillow,
sobbing, and I tremble all over. I
drink in small gulps of air, still alive,
and decide today I am sober

THE SAFE HAVEN

"Olly Olly in Free!"

— ANONYMOUS

Three words I never expected to say: "I love AA!"

Yet, here I am, sitting in a meeting one morning, feeling the weight of whatever trivial or overwhelming issues I carried in dissolve as soon as I find my seat. A wave of nostalgia washes over me, and I realize that this meeting is my "home fort."

Growing up as a Gen Xer, we spent our days outside, making adventures out of whatever we could find in the neigh-borhood. One of our favorite games was "War in the Woods." As kids, our imaginations ran wild, and the stakes felt real. The ultimate goal? Make it to the fort — or listen for the sweet, triumphant call of a teammate shouting, "Olly olly in free!"

AA is my fort. It's the place I run to when life's battles feel overwhelming, where I find safety in the midst of chaos. In this war of the real world, where the stakes are no longer just childhood games, that familiar call still rings true.

Olly olly in free!

The Daily Practice

A Shared Gratitude List
By Deborah W.

Today I will walk in gratitude for:

1. My morning routine, so set in stone, now leading me through whatever the day brings.
2. Being so busy with work and learning new things every day. The great relationship I'm building with my boss and coworkers. Love being part of a new growing business.
3. My kids helping pick up the slack at home.
4. Peace in my heart, finally, that everything will always be okay. I don't need a drug or alcohol to get through it anymore.
5. The many tools in my box and how very useful they are!
6. North Star Big Book, always hearing exactly what I need to hear, just like a meeting.
7. All my friends, sticking with the winners.

8. How important it is to reach out to other alcoholics every day and grateful for the big list of numbers I now have.

9. Being so very excited about the future, but remembering to stay in the moment and enjoy the ride.

10. My family, my home, Vida, my dog, the chickens, and my car. Having everything I need today.

The Storyteller

My niece, Sydney, won "story of the month" at her high school, and my sister-in-law shared it on social media. When I read it, I forgot it was written by a seventeen-year-old. She's a person without boundaries who has always been able to share honest emotion, and she loves herself completely. She loves so much, willingly shares anything she has, and is grateful for anything you give her.

When my liver failed, she was willing to give me part of hers, no questions asked. That's who she is.

After my surgery, I playfully asked if she wanted to see my scar, and she texted back "yes." So, I sent her a photo. "It makes you look badass," she replied.

For Christmas, we're having a blanket made for her so she can wrap up while she reads. It will be customized with four book titles, so I texted her to "Name four books, quick." She came back with "Holy Bible, the Torah, the Qu'Ran and a Harry Potter book."

This is her story.

A Snowman's Promise

By Sydney O'Blenes

"M-my snowman," a little boy's voice quivers upon seeing his once proud snowman melted into a puddle before him. The sight of the melted snow sparks the little boy's sorrow, and soon the puddle is more salt than water.

Slender, snow-white arms wrap around him. A mother's loving embrace, warm and caring. The little boy buries his head in the woman's stomach, tears staining her dress.

"Oh, my darling," She coos, softly running her hands in his hair, "Why are you crying?"

"My s-snowman..." he mutters forlornly, staring at his boots, wet with the remnants of his old friend.

The woman kneels on the piercing cold floor, hazel eyes staring into hazel eyes. Her arms wrap tighter around the boy, and he falls apart in her caress. Tears flow down his face, and the woman occasionally swipes away the droplets so they don't freeze on his plump little cheeks.

Once the boy's tears slow and his breathing evens out, she gives him one last squeeze before turning him around. "Look my darling, your friend isn't gone."

"Y-yes he is..." Confusion rings thick in his voice.

"No, my love, this is just the beginning of his life. Soon he'll be in the soil, in the breeze, feeding the birds in the trees. Bringing joy to the upcoming spring. But once the leaves of the trees start to crisp and Jack Frost starts to nip, your friend will be back."

He stares up at the woman, eyes wide with wonder, "B-but how, Mama?"

"All you have to do is believe. And when you build up the snow to see your friend next year, he'll be there."

"Promise, mama?"

She smiles, "I promise. Now go inside before you get frostbite."

The little boy trots back to his house, stomping the snow off his boots. He runs inside giggling with a newfound cheer.

"Why so chipper?" His father inquires with a smile.

"Mama said my snowman friend didn't leave me!"

His father's smile dims, "Baby, your mama couldn't have told you that …"

"No, she did," the boy says happily, "She told me, she told me!"

His father gets down on his knees. Tears threaten to spill from his eyes. "My boy, your mama has been asleep for years …"

The little boy's smile disappears. His lip quivers with fear. "B-but," His little face scrunches up with anger and confusion, "She told me, Papa! She's here!"

Nobody could convince the little boy that she was

gone. Winters came and went. Before he knew it, his own children were building snowmen with him. The boy, now a man, smiled at his children playing in the snow.

"Papa, Papa!" His little daughter came up smiling to hug his knee, "She's back!"

Her stout finger points at a beautiful young woman sitting on a tombstone next to their snowmen. The woman smiles lovingly, occasionally hugging her grandchildren.

The man's eyes go misty, as they do whenever she appears, "Mama, you came back!"

Getting Back to C.A.L.M

About ten years ago, a dear friend looked at me and said, "You know, you'd make a great life coach."

At the time, my ego probably thought, *Of course I would. I know everything.* Today, I know that only God is great. But I am a coach. And the little secret about recovery is that helping others is the ultimate key to staying sober.

It doesn't matter if I'm helping a guy move from the street to a shelter, from an apartment to a home, or even from a home to a mansion—it is intensely rewarding if I can be a part of it. (Though, for the record, I decline the guys who *only* want to be coached on getting a mansion. If they want to be coached on keeping their balance along the way? I'm their guy.)

I didn't add this chapter as a commercial for my business. I added it as an example of how this giant, loud ego of mine has actually been tamed. For decades, anything good that happened was my doing, and anything bad was someone else's fault, because—didn't you know?—I was fucking perfect.

This framework is how I survive my own brain today. (That being said, after you read it, if you want some coaching, I won't say no.)

This came about from reading *The Four Agreements* by Don Miguel Ruiz. I had heard about it for years, but I finally picked it up. The simplicity of those principles struck me. Not because they were complex, but because they were direct. They weren't about changing my world. They were about taking responsibility for how I show up inside of it.

I spent most of my life falling short of what I truly wanted because I spent my energy managing outcomes, controlling perceptions, correcting other people, or chasing validation. The agreements point inward instead. They ask: *What responsibility must I take to step forward and create the life I say I want?*

As I read, I found myself translating the ideas into the language I use to keep myself sober and sane. I wasn't trying to improve Ruiz's work; I was trying to make it practical for my own daily life—something that actually works in real conversations and real emotional moments.

What emerged is C.A.L.M.

Not calm as in passive. Not calm as in detached. C.A.L.M. as a way to step forward and live fully—humbly, and on my terms. Simple. Strong. Balanced.

I get in my own way when emotions rise, when conversations derail, and when assumptions begin running ahead of facts. For me, it's when my ego quietly steps in and starts trying to *win*, and I stop trying to *understand*. At work or at home, when these things happen, C.A.L.M. provides my reset. Because the real issue is rarely the moment itself, it's the gap between what I value and how I'm behaving.

Here is what C.A.L.M. looks like in my life:

C — Clean Communication

I have to start here. Before I analyze someone else's behavior, I have to examine my own words. I have to keep my side of the street clean. Clean means direct, honest, and free of exaggeration. No loaded language. No subtle manipulation. No insulting or over-talking just to "win." No saying one thing while meaning another. Clean communication reduces unnecessary drama. When conversations escalate, it is almost always because I am trying to score points instead of solving problems. Clean communication refuses to play that game. If something cannot be said cleanly yet, I might not be ready to say it.

A — About Me?

When someone reacts sharply, criticizes, withdraws, or disappoints me, my alcoholic brain moves quickly toward personalization. I immediately ask, "Why me?" or "What did I do?" Now, I force myself to pause and ask: *Is this actually about me?* Sometimes the answer is yes, and ownership matters. But usually, the answer is no. People operate from their own stress, fear, insecurity, and unresolved history. If I assume everything is about me, I end up carrying weight that was never mine to hold. Asking "About Me?" is not avoidance; it is accurate ownership. I am responsible for my actions. I am not responsible for managing everyone else's internal world. Refusing to take things personally keeps me steady.

L — Legacy Check

Assumptions rarely appear from nowhere. They come from accumulated history. A tone today can activate an old memory. A delay can feel like rejection because it once was. That is my legacy. A Legacy Check asks: *Am I responding to this moment, or to something from my past?* Without this check, old stories quietly narrate my new situations. I react as if history is repeating itself, even when it isn't. I step forward when I take each situation as it actually is—not as I fear it to be. When my legacy is left unchecked, assumptions feel like facts. When my legacy is examined, clarity returns.

M – Meaningful Effort

After I clean up my words, check my ego, and examine my history, I'm left with one question: *What would meaningful effort look like right now?* Not perfection. Not control. Not applause. Meaningful effort might be making an amends call. It might be staying quiet. It might be walking away instead of escalating. Meaningful effort is not measured the same every day. On my best days, I can't assume I'll repeat that same level of output tomorrow. The question isn't: *Did I perform at my highest level?* The question is: *Did I give an honest effort with what I had today?* I don't aim for flawless anymore. I aim for honesty.

C.A.L.M. isn't about controlling life. It is about governing myself. It is my reset tool. When I feel agitated, restless, discouraged, or overwhelmed—before I blame, defend, or withdraw—I return to the basics.

Swallowing My Own Medicine

On Thursday, I was waiting to pull into a parking spot for Mass. I wasn't running late. I had plenty of time. Life was a solid 8.

Then, I saw him.

A young guy in a dark hoodie was taking his time walking across the parking lot. He was moving at a pace I would describe as "way too leisurely for my liking." Immediately, the version of myself from before I entered long-term recovery—the guy with a very low tolerance for "inefficiency"—started screaming in the back of my head.

"Look at this guy," I thought. *"Probably has nowhere to go. No job. Get across the driveway! Some of us have a life!"*

Before finding recovery, that guy would have gotten a honk. On a bad day, I would've rolled down the window and unloaded. But today, I caught myself. I remembered the principle: *Principles before personalities.* I remembered that Jesus is in that kid just as much as He is in me. I said a Serenity Prayer for myself and a prayer for whatever was slowing him down.

Then, I drove past him.

As I got closer, I saw a massive ring of keys hanging from his belt loop—dozens of them, clinking against his leg. In a split second, my entire reality shifted. My brain did a 180-degree flip.

I didn't see a "bum" anymore. I thought, *"Oh, man. My bad. This guy must be incredibly important. Look at all those keys! He must run this whole place."*

I literally laughed out loud. Why did a ring of keys turn a stranger into a "superstar"?

Because of my Legacy.

When I was a kid in 1979, my social life was the church boys' choir. School was a struggle; I was a rotten student. But in that choir loft? I was an angel. And in that world, keys were the measure of a man's greatness. The older, respected guys had the keys to the loft, the music room, and the theatre.

I call this my Key Envy Madness. Even as I grew up, that legacy followed me. More keys equaled more value. Today, I have a car fob and one house key. I also have an A.A. chip on that ring. Those two things tell me I can always get into my home and I can always stay in my right mind.

But my Legacy Lens still tried to tell me that a stranger's value was tied to his keychain. I was making a wild assumption based on a story from forty years ago.

The Seating Chart Sabotage

It happened again today. A networking organizer texted: *"Please make sure you sit by Mr. X today."*

Immediately, the Legacy Lens slammed into place. My blood pressure went up. *"How dare she tell me where to sit! I'm a grown man."* I was already halfway down the road to playing small by being defensive.

That's when I pulled out the **A** from the framework: *About Me?* This is the stop-and-wait moment. Before I internalize, I have to ask: *Is this truly about me?* I forced myself to look at the facts versus the legacy.

The fact was, she was just organizing a meeting to be productive. The legacy? School seating charts. My Legacy Lens remembers being a kid and being told to sit where I was told based on being a "troublemaker." To my ten-year-old self, an assigned seat was a loss of freedom. It was a judgment on my character.

Once the *About Me?* circuit breaker did its work, I realized the assumption that she was "bossing me around" was just a ghost from a third-grade classroom. Once I got over myself, I could just be present for the meeting.

Checking My Lens

This is why I used to stay stuck at an 8. I would go through my day reacting to people who weren't really there. I judged the guy in the parking lot because of a story about keys. I got angry at a colleague because of a story about a school desk.

If I want to hit a 10, I have to do the work. I have to look at my Legacy and ask: *"Is my anger based on the facts of today, or the stories of my past?*

How is Recovery Like Bowling?

Recovery is serious business and sometimes hard to understand. I like to use analogies that can help us better understand our progress. When we break it into relatable pieces, like the steps involved in bowling, the journey becomes a little clearer.

For an alcoholic, recovery is not a game. There are no perfect games, no victory dances, and, definitely, no beer frames.

Bowling can sometimes be about luck, but sobriety is never about luck or chance. It's about hard work, commitment, and a willingness to change. Do the work, and the promises are guaranteed (Big Book pg. 83-84). These promises include freedom, happiness, and serenity for those who diligently follow the program.

The Big Book says, "Rarely have we seen a person fail who

has thoroughly followed our path." Success in recovery is not about random strikes but about consistently showing up and doing the work.

The Starting Line: Therapy.

Therapy is like the starting line of the bowling alley. It's where you prepare for the game, choose your ball, strategize, and start your throw. It's where you build awareness, process your emotions, and get the tools you need to approach sobriety with purpose and intention. Therapy helps you make sense of the game before you even step up to the lane.

Rolling the Ball: Your Actions.

Throwing the ball down the lane represents your actions. Every time you decide to show up for yourself—whether it's attending a meeting, reaching out for help, or simply getting through a challenging moment without drinking —you're rolling the ball without hitting the gutter. Some throws may feel perfect, while others might veer off course, but each one is part of your journey.

Spare, Strike, and the Perfect Game: Sobriety.

A spare represents progress, not perfection. You might not knock down every pin on the first roll, but you're still moving forward and picking yourself up after setbacks. A strike symbolizes working the steps and fully engaging in your recovery, making significant progress. And a 300? That's lifelong AA—the ultimate consistency and commitment to the process of staying sober.

The Bumpers: Recovery Coaching and The Ticket Angel.

Now, where does Recovery Coaching come in? Coaching can be the bumpers on the side of the lane, there to guide you and keep you from falling into the gutters. Sobriety isn't about being perfect; it's about staying in the lane and taking meaningful steps forward. Whether your coach is providing accountability, support, or tools to navigate challenges, they're there to make sure you keep moving toward your goals, frame by frame. Even LeBron has a coach.

To truly understand what it means to be a "bumper" for someone else, I have to take you back to a memory from long before I ever took my first drink.

Back in the day, Disneyland required separate tickets for each ride. The tickets were categorized from A to E, with E-tickets the best and reserved for the most thrilling attractions. You only got so many E-tickets in your ticket book, so you had to use them wisely.

The first time I went to Disneyland, I was a little older than most kids in SoCal taking their first trip—probably in first or second grade. I had carefully planned out my entire day, mapping our route and allocating our precious E-tickets to the best rides. The first stop was the Haunted Mansion. When we got in line, I reached for my ticket book—and it was gone. Someone had stolen it.

We didn't have enough money to buy more tickets. My day, my week—my entire young life—felt ruined. I was devastated and broke into tears. I had read all about the Haunted Mansion's special effects, and now I was going to miss everything. The summer sun felt unbearably hot, the once-sweet smells of the park turned into the sweat and tears of a crying child, and the tombstones that had amused me moments before now seemed dark and ominous. The grey surrounding me felt like a real cemetery, not a Disney ride.

Then, suddenly, a woman's hand touched my shoulder. This beautiful hand offered me a brand-new ticket book and said, "I think you dropped this."

Like an angel, she saved my trip. To this day, I don't know if she had found my actual book or simply gave me a spare, but she expected nothing in return. She was just one human being helping another. I am not sure if she felt sorry for me or pitied my poor mom, who was dealing with an out-of-control, blubbering child, but this earthly angel saved my first trip to Disneyland. A total stranger made it "The Happiest Place on Earth" for real.

This woman could have kept the tickets for her own family. She could have tried to sell them to my mom for a bit less than full price since we were obviously desperate. But, instead, this blessed stranger gave me the tickets.

That act of kindness left an imprint on me, instilling in me at a very young age the desire to help others and do the right thing. Sorry to my atheist and agnostic friends that you may miss the glory of God in this memory.

That woman was a bumper. She saw a kid heading straight for the gutter, and she stepped in to keep my life on the lane, expecting zero credit.

In recovery, that is exactly what we do for each other.

DOWNSIDES OF THE BOWLING ALLEY FOR ALCOHOLICS

While the bowling alley can be an excellent metaphor for recovery, it also mirrors the real challenges that alcoholics face. The bar in the front of the alley is a glaring temptation—always there, always stocked, and often the centerpiece of the experience for many. The sound of clinking beer bottles or the casual offers of "just one drink" can be hard to ignore.

The game can be an emotional rollercoaster. If you're playing poorly or striking out frame after frame, frustration and self-criticism can lead to negative thoughts. Playing well can be just as risky. Success might spark overconfidence or a false belief that you're "cured," making it easier to justify a drink.

Social dynamics can add to the struggle. Flirting, competitiveness, or disagreements can spark emotions that you may have habitually numbed with alcohol. Anger over a bad game or someone else's behavior might bring out old coping mechanisms, like storming off or reaching for a drink. Even the environment itself—the smell of beer, loud music, or rowdy patrons—can trigger memories of past drinking binges, making the bowling alley both a symbol of fun and a minefield of potential setbacks.

In recovery, these triggers are opportunities to build healthier coping mechanisms—setting boundaries, practicing mindfulness, and leaning on a support network to navigate difficult moments.

PULLING IT ALL TOGETHER

The bowling alley is like recovery. It's a place full of opportunities to grow, succeed, and embrace life's joys—all while staying focused on what truly matters. But it comes with challenges and temptations. The key is learning to navigate both the strikes and the gutter balls, the cheers and the distractions, and stay focused on the lane in front of you, one day at a time.

Sobriety is much more critical than bowling. It's not about hitting a perfect score every time but about showing up, taking the shot, and learning from each roll. With the proper support, therapy, AA, sponsorship, and coaching, you can stay in the game and keep progressing toward the life you deserve.

So, lace up those shoes and step onto the lane. Your next throw is an opportunity to get closer to your goals.

Question: What are the "gutters" in your own life, and how do you avoid them while keeping your focus on the pins that matter most?

WHAT RECOVERY MEANS TO ME

Recovery isn't just about putting the bottle down. It's about picking life back up with both hands, shaky as they may be. It's about waking up without shame and going to bed with a little pride. It's about learning to sit with myself, no soundtrack, no escape hatch, and be okay with the guy in the mirror.

It's not a straight line, and it sure as hell isn't one-size-fits-all.

Recovery is learning how to sit with pain without trying to numb it. It's showing up for myself and for others even when I don't feel like it. It's about making amends where I can, forgiving where I need to, and learning to laugh again… really laugh, not that fake, "I'm fine" laugh that used to mask the mess.

Recovery means rewriting the story I told myself—that I wasn't enough, that I'd already blown it, that the damage was done. It means replacing self-loathing with self-respect, secrecy with honesty, and isolation with connection. It means forgiving myself without letting myself off the hook.

In AA, they say, "Listen, and you'll hear your story." I never listened. Not really. I had what they call a "high bottom." I was still working, still functioning—until a medical diagnosis pulled the rug out. And I worked in the liquor business, which added an extra layer of denial and irony.

Then one day, at a meeting at Mission Santa Ynez, I heard a guy share about buying a winery to cover his drinking. I almost laughed out loud. I didn't hear my exact story, but I heard something close enough to crack me open. That was the moment I understood the power of sharing.

Fast-forward, and I found myself comforting a newcomer who was crushed after leaving her bartending job. I didn't give her advice—I gave her *me*. I shared what it felt like to walk away from a career steeped in booze and identity. And I reminded her that leaving isn't the end. It's the beginning of something better.

That's when I realized that recovery isn't just achieving sobriety. It's about sharing the gift of sobriety with others.

Alcoholics with some sobriety under our belts know that recovery isn't a solo journey. We don't preach. We partner. We don't fix. We walk beside. We don't show up with capes or clipboards. We show up with lived experience, a steady presence, and the kind of honesty that cuts through the noise.

We've walked the walk—through the fog, the fear, the false starts—and we remember how overwhelming those early days were. So, we lead with empathy, not ego. The tools we've picked up—accountability, emotional regulation, boundary setting, self-compassion—weren't learned in a classroom. They were earned through trial, error, and showing up when we least wanted to.

We don't use them to tell others what to do. We use them to model what's possible. Whether it's through sponsorship, informal mentoring, or just being present in a meeting, we try to be the kind of support we needed when we were just starting out. Because if we could turn our lives around after years—even decades—of self-destruction, there's hope for anyone.

Recovery means learning to be the kind of parents, partners, friends, and humans we always meant to be. Even if we fall short, we show up. We laugh more. Cry when we need to. And recognize that growth doesn't come with a finish line.

And above all, recovery means gratitude. Every damn day.

So… What does recovery mean to you—today?

A Couple of Sober Reflections

Step Five: God Already Knows

Before we dive into this first reflection, let me give a quick crash course for the "normies" out there reading this—the folks who haven't had to sit in folding chairs and drink bad coffee to save their own lives.

In Alcoholics Anonymous, Step Four requires you to write down a searching and fearless moral inventory of your life. Basically, you make a master list of all your resentments, fears, and the exact nature of your screw-ups. It is a terrifying piece of paper.

Then comes Step Five, which states: "Admitted to God, to ourselves, and to another human being the exact nature of our wrongs." That means you have to sit down and actually read that list out loud to someone else. You can't just keep it locked in your head. It is one of the hardest things you will ever do. But here is the catch...

Because, for this alcoholic, Step Five isn't about informing God.

That realization didn't come to me in a meeting or a workbook. It came to me at Catholic Mass, of all places — during one of those call-and-response moments I used to say on autopilot when I was a child. A few weeks ago, the response was: "You have searched me, and you know me, Lord."

I said it. I said it again, I said it again, and one more time.

Then I paused.

Then I thought, *Well... that's inconvenient, but so very true!* (I did text it to a few friends, too).

And because it's true — and I believe it is — then God already knows what I've done. Not just the highlight reel or the sanitized version, but the whole thing. No omissions. No foot-notes. No explanations about why I was under a lot of stress, or drunk, or mad at so-and-so at the time.

Then I thought of my program and if God already knows, why does Step Five ask me to admit "to God, to ourselves, and to another human being the exact nature of our wrongs"?

Because, for me, Step Five isn't about giving God new infor-mation. It's about making sure *I* have the info.

God knows. I'm the one who forgets, minimizes, edits, reframes, or flat-out avoids.

Step Five forces me to stop negotiating with reality. It's not about shame — it's about ownership. Saying out loud, with another human being present, "Yes. This is mine. That is part of me."

Step Five isn't meant to make me feel terrible; it's meant to hold me accountable.

The Confession

Early in my sobriety, I returned to the Catholic Church, and I found myself thinking: *It's time for my first confession in forty years.* That sentence alone could've had me running in the other direction.

Confession and Step Five look similar from a distance. Both involve honesty. Both involve another person. Both involve admitting things I'd rather keep in my head. But they are not the same conversation — and I don't think they're meant to be.

In Step Five, the other person isn't standing *in* for God. They're standing *with* me. The point is to be seen as human, by a human, without collapsing or defending myself. For me, my sponsor, whose Higher Power isn't even the same God as mine, was the man for this role.

Confession is different. In the sacrament, the priest isn't just another person — he's acting in a specific role, within a specific structure, offering absolution that doesn't depend on his opinion of me or my storytelling skills.

That's why, for me, during confession, my priest can't replace the "Other Person" in Step Five.

But — and this matters — a priest *can* absolutely be a Fifth Step listener *outside* the sacrament. In that setting, he's not absolving. He's witnessing. He's listening. He's helping me stay honest without the conversation becoming transactional.

Two different conversations. Two different purposes. Both necessary.

When I finally went to confession, I wasn't telling the priest anything God didn't already know. What I was doing was removing my last exit ramp. I was saying the truth without qualifiers.

After I finished, the priest gave me my penance and then added, very calmly, that part of my penance was to say my assigned prayers on my knees. I believe that suggestion landed exactly where it was supposed to.

It didn't feel like punishment. It felt like a diagnosis. God knew and made it so the priest could see that while my drinking had been knocked flat, my ego was still doing light stretching. Kneeling put that last bit of ego in check! At least for now.

Doing that penance wasn't for God. God didn't need convincing. It was for me — because self-forgiveness requires participation.

Then the priest said something else that surprised me. He told me that the closer I grow in my faith, the more aware I'll likely become of my sins and defects.

Before I could stop myself, I said, "Well, I'm an alcoholic. I've done a Fourth Step. I've already got about 144 defects if you want to see the list."

He smiled, but he did not ask for the list. That signaled to me that what I am guilty of isn't as important as wanting to repent. (Drifting into Step Six).

What he said next stuck with me. He explained that growth doesn't erase defects — it increases awareness. The light gets brighter. The details sharpen. What once blended into the background becomes visible.

At first, that sounded difficult, because I thought progress was supposed to mean *less* wrong with me, not a higher-resolution image of it. But that hasn't been my experience in sobriety either.

Early recovery gave me fewer fires to put out. Ongoing recovery gives me better eyesight to see the defects.

Step Five didn't make me perfect, and confession didn't make me spotless. What they gave me was alignment.

What I say matches what I know. What I know matches how I live. And when it doesn't, I notice faster — and course-correct sooner. Shame thrives in the dark, but accountability thrives in the light.

God already knew everything on my list. The difference is that now, I do too.

And once I stopped pretending otherwise — once I stood in the truth with another human being, and then again on my knees — I found something I didn't expect.

Not judgment. Not punishment. But relief.

Because being fully known — by God, by another person, and finally by myself — turns out not to be the threat I feared.

It's the beginning of freedom.

The Christ Cathedral Awakening

Some places are more than buildings. They become characters in the story of your life.

For me, a place like that is Christ Cathedral in Garden Grove, CA.

Long before it was a Catholic Cathedral, it was the Crystal Cathedral—one of the most famous churches in America, built by televangelist Robert H. Schuller. Like many people in Southern California, I grew up aware of it. But I never imagined how often my life would intersect with that shimmering glass sanctuary.

As a teenager, I played handbells in my Catholic parish choir. We were invited to play weddings at the Crystal Cathedral, and I remember walking into that immense glass space with bells in hand, sunlight pouring through thousands of panes of glass. At the time, it simply felt impressive. I didn't realize I was stepping into a place that would quietly be with me as I stepped through decades of life.

Years later, when my own family was growing, I bought some tickets for a bunch of us as a Christmas gift so we could all attend the famous Christmas Pageant together. If you ever saw it, you know what it was like.

It was spectacular.

Live animals. Massive choirs. Dramatic lighting. And at one point, angels—actual humans suspended high above the sanctuary—flying through the air while singing. It felt like something between a Broadway show and a worship service.

For a long time, the cathedral seemed larger than life.

Then came the difficult years.

Like many large ministries, the church faced struggles—financial pressures, leadership changes, and family challenges that unfolded very publicly. None of that erases the good the ministry did for many people, but it was a painful chapter. Eventually, the campus went through bankruptcy, and for a time, the future of the great glass cathedral was uncertain.

For several years, it sat mostly quiet.

Then something remarkable happened.

The campus was purchased by the Roman Catholic Diocese of Orange and began a long transformation into Christ Cathedral. The building that had once symbolized American televangelism would become the center of Catholic worship in Orange County.

But the most remarkable part of the story was unfolding just across the street.

Directly across from the cathedral campus sits a Kaiser Addiction Medicine Clinic. That is where I eventually found myself sitting in a recovery group led by a therapist who specializes in cirrhosis and alcohol recovery.

In that building—literally across the street from the cathedral altar—my life was saved.

At the time, I wasn't thinking about symbolism or geography. I was just trying to survive alcoholism and learn how to live again.

Only later did it strike me.

The place where my recovery began was less than a football field away from the altar where I now attend Mass.

As a teenager, I rang bells inside that sanctuary. As an adult, I brought my family there for Christmas celebrations. And years later, after returning to the Catholic Church, I attended my first Christmas Mass back in my religion there, at that historic place. It wasn't technically midnight Mass. It was the 3:00 PM family Mass. But to me, it might as well have been midnight.

Recently, a Christian friend from A.A. asked if I would take him to see the cathedral. He knew I went to Mass there weekly, and he had heard how beautiful the building was and wanted to visit, though he made it clear he didn't want to attend a Catholic Mass. I was happy to show off the grand place. I welcomed the chance to share the space with him. I've reached a place in my life where I see the beauty in every path to the light – it's a gift available to anyone who seeks it, regardless of where or how they pray. To me, the walls of the cathedral aren't there to keep people out, but to hold a space where anyone—Catholic or not —can feel a little closer to their faith.

As we walked through the campus, the roar of Chapman Avenue traffic seemed to dissolve. The air felt different there— stilled by the sound of the fountains and the wide, open plazas. We stepped inside, and for a moment, we both just stood there. The light poured through the thousands of glass "petals" on the walls, creating a shimmering, underwater glow that felt both immense and intimate.

The space was alive with quiet movement. We watched people scattered throughout the pews; some were deep in silent meditation, while others stood before the statues of the saints, their lips moving in whispered petitions. My friend watched them with a quiet curiosity. He didn't quite understand our Catholic tradition of honoring the saints or "talking" to the statues, but he didn't need to. He recognized the universal language of devotion. He saw that they weren't praying to stone, but reaching out to something far greater, using the art around them as a bridge.

Right then, the air began to vibrate. Someone was at the great Hazel Wright Organ, practicing for a service. A single voice began to sing, the notes climbing up into the glass rafters and hanging there like incense. It wasn't a performance; it was just a moment of pure, unforced beauty.

My friend stood there, taking it all in for a long moment. Finally, he leaned over and said softly, *"I can feel something in this place."* The experience hadn't just impressed him; it had moved him.

In that moment, I realized the cathedral had quietly become a character in my life's story.

It was there when I was young. It was there when my family gathered in joy. It was there through years of uncertainty and change. And it was standing just across the street when I found the help that saved my life.

Sometimes we imagine grace arriving in dramatic ways. But in this case, the distance between where my recovery began and where I now attend Mass weekly is only a few hundred feet.

Sometimes grace doesn't travel very far. Sometimes it's waiting right across the street.

Deeper Gratitude

HELLO AGAIN. IT'S BEEN FIVE MONTHS SINCE I LAST worked on this book. From where I sit, the dogs have easy access for cuddles, and I can see Christmas Tree Two next to the TV. Christmas Tree two is our fun tree, filled with ornaments from family members — scuba divers from my brother, a lot of "sister" ornaments from Missy's sister, and three Captain Americas. Stockings hang on the fireplace, which is surrounded by festive holly. Pots of white poinsettias with cranberries are on the bookshelves, and a small nativity scene is in front of the TV. Two angels kiss on a side table. Missy's mother adored those angels, so Missy and her sister trade them back and forth each Christmas season because they were so special to her. I can see a framed Kinkade Christmas print in the kitchen and Missy's childhood felt Advent Calendar. We take turns pinning objects on it each day, counting down to Christmas.

I didn't stop writing for six months because I got lazy, but because I got distracted — though, you could argue they're the same thing. I think about that a lot when alcoholics skip meetings, effectively blowing off their own sobriety. The Twelve Steps and Twelve Traditions tell us that AA unity is the single most important piece of our sobriety — even before our own actions. I recently came across this gem while studying the traditions with my sponsor:

"The unity of Alcoholics Anonymous is the most cherished quality our society has." 12 Steps and 12 Traditions, p. 129, 4th edition

Without the AA fellowship, most of us don't stay sober. The message must be shared — not by TV shows or celebrities, but by us, the common folk. So, if you're supposed to be going to meetings, I suggest you go. Not just for yourself, but to support the fellowship. It's good for the world.

I was distracted from writing because I had a liver transplant. Yep, brand new, fully functioning liver. A miracle. A blessing. I thank God every day for my health, for my wife's ability to nurse me back to strength, and for the family of the liver donor. Since the transplant, I've meditated and prayed for that family. And a few weeks ago, I had an awakening about the difficulty — and divinity — of organ donation.

But first, let's acknowledge the miracle of medical science. The process of organ transplantation is incredible. When you read that, you probably nodded in agreement, maybe you smiled, felt a little hope, a little pride in humanity. Well, a miracle is God at work. Atheists and men of science might call my faith quaint, but from where I sit, it's quaint that they don't see the blessing they've been given. Their skill, their dedication, the years of study, the long hours, the cost, the single-minded purpose—are all a blessing. A gift. Thank you, Lord, for our healers.

At an AA meeting, I had an awakening about donor families. A new face was in the room, a woman sitting near the open door. The sun shone in on her like a spotlight from heaven. She was dressed like most of us in jeans and a t-shirt. When it was her turn to share, she spoke through tears about her twenty-two-year-old stepdaughter who had been killed by a drunk driver over the weekend. The room held its breath. Then, she told us the hospital asked her family to keep their daughter on life support for ten days so they could find recipients for her organs. The pain on her face said it all. She couldn't sit still, fidgeted with the book in front of her, covered her mouth to contain her anger, and avoided everyone's eyes.

During my transplant journey, the doctors and nurses constantly reminded me to pray for the family of my donor. But until that moment, I'd never truly considered what those families endure — the unfathomable loss, then the agonizing decision to keep their loved one's body alive solely to save strangers. I always knew organ donation was a divine gift, but I'd never fully grasped the strength it required. When these people have just endured the worst loss imaginable, they're asked to prolong their loved one's lifeless body to help people like me. Only our Creator can fully comprehend a mystery like that. We can't see everything, but I accept that whatever is happening is exactly as it's supposed to be.

When it was my turn, I thanked the woman. I told her that as a transplant recipient, although I couldn't imagine her pain, I was deeply grateful for the unselfish choice her family had made. I let her know that a stranger's generosity had given me the beauty of a second chance at life. Knowing about the person who passed — and now, understanding the extra pain their family suffered — only strengthened my resolve never to drink again. Never to damage the gift I'd been given. She thanked me for my words, but I could tell she wasn't really seeing me. She looked straight through me. I understand now. She heard me, but her brain couldn't process it.

The next week, we were at the same meeting. This time, she shared that her stepdaughter's organs had saved the lives of eight people. Once again, I thanked her and her family for their impossible decision and told her that I'd shared her story with the people in my liver transplant support group, who were all moved to tears. We recognized the depth of her family's sacrifice. We saw them not just as kind, but as modern superheroes. I told her that her family's actions hadn't just saved eight lives. They had touched hundreds. After my share, she looked me in the eyes for the first time. She said thank you. And I could see that, finally, she was beginning to understand not what her family had lost, but the magnitude of the gift they'd given.

With Missy's support, I decided to make a living amends to other addicts by founding a recovery coaching service: Living Step Solutions. My idea is that our coaches would act as bumpers on the bowling alley of sobriety. Our therapy sessions would be the place where you pick up your ball, keep score, and get ready to play. I thought of taking action, doing the work, as rolling the ball. Joining AA or another twelve-step program, staying sober, and helping others would earn you a strike, while a split would require a strong game plan to pick it up. I hope the analogy works for you. If you want more details, check out my blog, Sobriety Like a Bowling Alley atwww.livingstepsolutions.com. Starting the business took time, but now that everything's in place, I return to writing with more gratitude for the gift of life than I've ever felt.

Thankful vs. Grateful: A Reflection on My Journey

The journey through recovery is filled with lessons. Lately, I've been thinking about the difference between being thankful and being grateful. For a long time, I didn't give much thought to those words. They seemed interchangeable. But as I've worked the steps and walked my path, I've come to realize they mean different things, especially in the context of recovery.

When I first found out I needed a liver transplant, I was upset, overwhelmed, and unsure how to cope. Drinking wasn't an option anymore, and for the first time in a long while, I had to face my emotions head-on. In those early moments, I decided to focus on what I could be thankful for and told myself to be thankful that a surgery existed to save my life. But gratitude came later, and it ran deeper. To qualify for the transplant, I had to be sober for six months. At the time, it felt like just another hoop to jump through, another test in a series of challenges. But looking back, I'm grateful for those six months of sobriety, because they became the foundation for something much bigger. They gave me a chance at recovery, and I pray that that six-month requirement will become a lifetime of sobriety. Moments like those remind me that thankfulness and gratitude are intertwined. Being thankful got me through those early days. Being grateful keeps me moving forward.

When I think about being thankful, I think of specific moments when someone showed up for me, or life handed me a break I didn't see coming. After my surgery, my wife became my caregiver. She stepped up in ways I'll never be able to fully repay. I'm thankful for her selflessness during those long, challenging days. But my gratitude is even more profound. I'm grateful that we found each other. She's beautiful both outside and inside, and her strength and kindness have carried me through some of life's hardest moments. I don't take it for granted that I share my life with a woman like her in good times and bad.

I see the same distinction in so many moments of my life today. Recently, friends invited me to a family gathering, and I felt thankful to be included. As I sat there surrounded by people who truly cared, asked how I was doing, and genuinely listened, it hit me how much deeper my feelings went. I wasn't just thankful for the invitation; I was grateful for the people who have come into my life and for the connections that continue to grow and support me in recovery. I'm thankful that I can attend AA meetings, that there's a safe space to share and learn. But my gratitude is for the worldwide fellowship of AA. No matter where I go, I know I'll find people who understand and speak the same language of hope and recovery. Before I began this journey, I didn't know I needed that gift.

I'm thankful for my sponsor, whose guidance has been invaluable as I work the twelve steps, but my gratitude extends beyond him. I'm grateful for all those who walked this road before me and laid the foundation and shared their wisdom and stories so people like me could have a chance at a better life.

Looking back, I see so many moments where thankfulness and gratitude intertwine. Before recovery, I was too wrapped up in my own struggles, too caught in the cycle of shame and regret to see them. But today, I try to honor them. I remind myself to thank the people who make a difference in my life and to pause and reflect on the bigger picture, the gifts that come from a power greater than myself, which I believe is the God of the Bible. For me, this creates an ever-growing list that keeps me grounded and hopeful.

What are you thankful for today? And what are you grateful for in the grander scheme of things? I suggest you write these things down, then refer to the list regularly and add to it. Be mindfully thankful and grateful for at least a few minutes every day.

I review my master list every single night to keep myself grounded. But the practice doesn't stop there. I also write a separate, new gratitude list every evening that I share with others in recovery. It keeps the gratitude fresh, it keeps me accountable, and it keeps me connected.

This is my current master grateful list:

- **I live a God-centered life:** I know and love God. He is in control, and I am just one of his kids. Reading the Gospel daily and reflecting with Tim, Vince, and Jim.

- **2 ½ years plus of sobriety.**

- **Missy:** Our relationship is priceless and almost perfect. I wouldn't change a thing. She has improved her work/home balance, and I am so grateful for how much she loves me.

- **I am alive:** My new liver was a quick wait time, perfect surgery, and quick recovery with no setbacks. For the family whose loved one passed, and gave life to strangers. The previous owner of my liver.

- **The medical team:** The doctors and nurses who kept me alive. Dr. McClune.

- **Living Step Solutions:** I passed my classes to start Living Step Solutions. I have earned many certificates. I am a Certified Professional Coach (CPC), Recovery Coach, and Certified Peer Support Specialist.

- **My purpose:** I have created two apps to help people keep on track. I get to help people, and that service helps me stay sober.

- **Health and Clarity:** I am healthy with an excellent medical team. Mayo/Kaiser. My thinking is back to normal - clear.

- **Adventures:** I can go on vacation and go SCUBA diving.

- **Dear friends:** I have dear friends - Tim and Kay, John, Mark, Michael, Leena, Terry, and America.

- **Future:** I have a retirement plan that works.

- **Family:** Emily is finding her true self.

- **Hobbies:** My outdoor kitchen. That I am getting back to enjoying, I am reading and writing more.

- **My sober support family:** Jody, John, Javier, Kurtis, Mark, Krista, Debbie K., A.A., Kaiser.

- **Sponsees:** I have two great sponsees to help my sobriety.

- **Puppies:** I have great puppies - love them, and they love back!

A Story of Gratitude from My Past

Gratitude has a way of reshaping the way we see our past. It highlights the good, even in the things we once took for granted. Before sobriety, before the transplant, some of my most treasured experiences revolved around fine food and wine. At the time, I thought I was savoring life. Looking back, I see those moments differently, not just for what was in my glass, but for the company, the atmosphere, and the memories made. This story takes me back to those times, with a perspective that has deepened.

My life once revolved around wine — not just drinking it, but understanding it, appreciating its nuances, and immersing myself in the culture surrounding it. I was a "wine guy" by profession and passion. That identity took me to some of the world's most legendary wine cellars, from Graycliff in Nassau, Bahamas, to Tour d'Argent in Paris; the walls in those places held history, and bottles older than I was. Today, as the founder of Living Step Solutions, my relationship with those memories has changed. But the stories remain worth telling.

My wife and I made lunch reservations at Tour d'Argent, one of the most storied restaurants in Paris, with a history dating to the sixteenth century. Before heading out, we casually mentioned our plans to the concierge at our hotel. We were dressed in daytime tourist clothes, and she absolutely insisted that we change. That should've given us a clue. When we arrived, properly dressed, we were greeted with an elegant "Henri?"—the French pronunciation of Henry. But as soon as I opened my mouth, the staff's expressions sagged. Americans! We were promptly escorted to the worst table in the house, in the middle of the dining room, as far as possible from the panoramic windows that framed a spectacular view of the Seine and Notre Dame. We might as well have been in a basement.

I attempted to ask, "Can we—" but before I could even finish my sentence, the maître d' cut me off with a firm, "No! You sit here!" So, we sat, and I did what any self-respecting wine professional would do. I asked for the wine list. I had no idea. The menu they handed me was larger than a phone book, a thick, leather-bound volume that could double as weightlifting equipment. If you're under the age of thirty and don't know what a phone book is, imagine trying to carry an entire set of encyclopedias — yes, those were a thing, too. When I couldn't lift it, I relented and accepted help from one of the three sommeliers hovering around the room. I was an alcoholic, and it was lunchtime in Paris, so I ordered three half bottles for the two of us.

While chatting with the sommelier, I casually mentioned my background in the wine industry, and the temperature in the room changed. I was no longer just an American tourist. I was one of them. When we finished our entrées, the staff invited us to tour the cellar. The Tour d'Argent is one of the most storied in the world, sparkling with hidden gems. As we descended the steps, we felt we were stepping into a secret world. The temperature and humidity were controlled for the sake of the wine, not human comfort, so they wrapped my wife in a fur coat. This labyrinth of history was filled with mold — deep, necessary, and colorful — clinging to bottles aged beyond memory. But the most striking details were in the brick walls that exposed a façade built hastily during World War II to hide the wine from the Nazis. Standing among bottles that had survived war, occupation, and decades of history was a humbling moment, reminding me that wine wasn't just about drinking. It's a legacy.

When we emerged from the cellar, something had changed. The maître d' who had so firmly seated us at our "middle of nowhere" table had relocated us — not just to a better table, but to the best seat in the house, overlooking the Seine on one side and Notre Dame on the other, a view worthy of royalty. It was a once-in-a-lifetime experience. We even bought a book about the famed restaurant. It's in French so we can't read it, but it's still displayed in our living room. Luckily, it was a lunch, so I managed to stay sober enough to remember every detail.

Years later, I toured the legendary Graycliff Wine Cellar in Nassau, Bahamas. Unlike Tour d'Argent, the magic wasn't in the historic walls, but in the labels themselves, bottles I'd never seen before, legends of the wine world, including a vertical of Château d'Yquem spanning over twenty years. Château d'Yquem is a premier Sauternes, a dessert wine so refined and complex it's been known to age for a century or more. Seeing those bottles, I felt like a historian stumbling upon the original Declaration of Independence.

But — and it is a big but — alcohol is cunning, baffling,

and powerful. It always brings an alcoholic to the dark side. There's another side to the grandeur and romance of those moments. For an alcoholic, love of wine becomes something else entirely, a place where indulgence blurs into dependence, where experiences became excuses to drink more, and where even the most exquisite bottles can't mask the damage you're doing to yourself. At the time, I justified it. It was part of my career, part of my passion. But looking back, I see how easy it was to let the culture of drinking consume me and turn something refined into something reckless. Drinking destroyed me and left its mark on those around me, strained relationships, eroded trust, and obscured precious moments in a fog of intoxication.

A Perspective on Sobriety

Looking back, I recognize how easy it was to romanticize drinking and reminisce about the way wine elevated those moments. But the best parts of those stories have nothing to do with alcohol. It wasn't the wine that made the Tour d'Argent cellar fascinating; it was the history hidden in its walls. It wasn't the grand cru that made Greycliff special; it was seeing bottles that had endured decades, even centuries, silent witnesses to history. And it certainly wasn't the alcohol that made the maître d' move us to the best seat in the house. It was connection, shared passion, and human experience.

That's what I carry forward in sobriety. Alcohol didn't make these experiences special; life did. And life, even at its most refined, elevated moments, is just as extraordinary without a drop of wine. For those in recovery, it's important to recognize that our memories are ours to keep. We don't need to erase or deny the richness of our past experiences; we just need to acknowledge them with honesty. That honesty includes recognizing both the beauty and the damage. It means remembering not just the charm of our drinking days, but also the chaos, the hurt we caused, and the ways alcohol distorted what could have been even better moments. The key is to separate nostalgia from temptation and recognize that while alcohol was present in those moments, it was never the thing that made them great. I promise you, alcohol never made anything better. Today, I enjoy travel, fine dining, and memories — not through a wine glass, but through clear eyes, an open heart, and the knowledge that the best seat in the house is always the one where I can be truly present and sober.

My Son's Shitty Father

Before we get into this, I need to make an admission.

The person I was representing and writing from in the first few chapters of this book was a real asshole. I have to acknowledge that was me. That guy couldn't possibly admit what is coming in this chapter.

Being able to acknowledge what I am about to share isn't something I am proud of, nor is it something I can change. But my experience might help others. This is one of the promises of A.A. coming true, and a perfect example of that divine program at work. You see, stopping drinking is one thing, but being able to write this chapter? That is *recovery*.

It is coming full circle from the guy who would fight you over a proper martini and protect his right to be right at all costs. From a guy who would say everything was someone else's fault, to a guy looking in the mirror and saying: My most important job, I fucked up. I truly am a shitty father.

Alcoholism isn't a failure. It's a disease. But being a terrible father isn't a disease. It's a failure.

I wasn't a good father to my son, Paul, and I can't blame that on my alcoholism. It started long before I was drinking heavily. I could give you a hundred reasons why, but in the end, they're just excuses. Even now, thirty-seven years later, I'm only slightly better at fathering.

The Cambridge Dictionary defines fatherhood as "the state or time of being a father." I was never in a state of being a father. I was in a state of denial. The single most important job I had was being Paul's father, and I refused to acknowledge it. I was too busy trying to build a career in the restaurant business. I didn't have time for something as trivial as raising my own child. I didn't take care of him. I barely played with him. I certainly didn't love him the way he deserved to be loved. The poor kid never had a chance. I was lazy, selfish, and incapable of unconditional love.

With the pressures of a newborn, a new job, and moving back to our hometown from Ashland, Oregon, where Paul was born, I stopped paying attention to his mother, too. Then I met a server at work who seemed more fun than a wife and kid. Paul's mother and I separated. I didn't have an affair, but I wanted to. I was a self-centered, egomaniacal narcissist, thinking only about myself. We married too young. My friends warned me, but I was the center of my own universe, and I didn't listen. A marriage counselor told us, "Your communication is great.

You just don't like each other very much." That sums it up. Paul's mother and I came from broken homes. We learned how to be a couple from watching TV shows where couples fight all the time. I thought that was love.

When Paul was still young, his mother met a fine gentleman who has been good to Paul for thirty-five years, and I appreciate that. At a time when I was nowhere near the man I am now, Paul and his mother moved to Seattle to be with this man. Now I'd fight to keep him in this state, but then I fought tooth and nail to pay as little child support as possible. I was so self-centered that I deprived my son to spite his mother. Luckily for her — and for Paul — her new husband did well financially. I hate to admit that part of me was relieved when Paul went to live with them. He'd never want for anything, and the burden of day-to-day parenting was no longer mine. I was a total, undeniable dick. That was one of the first concrete decisions I made in my cycle of poor fathering. If I had fought as hard to keep Paul in my life as I did to avoid paying for him, who knows what might have happened?

I can't change the past, but I don't regret it. I've made amends to my son for that poor decision, and I recognize it for what it was. Every time his mother asked for extra money for a gift or anything beyond basic child support, I said no. I wasn't denying her. I was denying Paul. Before they moved to Seattle, I was allowed to spend time with Paul every other weekend and every Wednesday. In the early years, those were good times, but I was playing at being a dad. His mother did all the heavy lifting. I was the parsley on the plate. I had a connection that got us into Disneyland for free, and we went so often that after a while, Paul was more interested in the gift shops than the rides. We spent most Thanksgivings together and decorated the Christmas tree the day after. One year, that stopped abruptly. I honestly don't remember why. I sent Christmas presents every year. Somehow, I also got shoe duty. When he visited in the summer, I'd buy him a new pair of sneakers. I knew it was his mother's way of getting me to contribute extra money. I was so self-centered.

Paul flew to me for summer breaks. Eventually, when I got to the airport, I could tell which passengers were visiting Southern California and which were coming home. The returnees had a healthy glow and energy. The visitors from Seattle, where the sun barely shines, were pasty with a greenish tint. It was like watching swamp people come off the plane. No wonder Seattle has high suicide rates.

Once when I picked Paul up, I was met by a very angry flight attendant who informed me that he'd been awful. I asked, "How bad could he be?" She held up her hand to show me where he bit her. My kid had full-on chomped her hand. Thank God she was kind enough not to press charges or ban him from flying. I don't remember punishing him. I just told him not to do it again, and, like the excellent role model I was, agreed with him that the flight attendant was a bitch. A therapist could write a book about my delusions. I thought I was being "good" to him so he'd love me.

The Camp

As Paul grew, so did his behavioral issues. I hate to admit it, but I can't give you a lot of details because I wasn't there. I was hundreds of miles away, praying I wouldn't get a call from his mom about his latest misstep. Rather than step up and help, I sat on the sidelines and watched my son struggle with mental health issues his mother couldn't handle alone. I'm confident that his mother and I contributed to every one of those issues. Occasionally, I'd make a trip up north and see my son, which sounds nice, but I only went when I had business in Seattle. I'd spend a couple of hours with him while I was there. I was a bum.

On one of my visits, he'd been grounded. His mother always felt bad for grounding him and bought him a new video game to make up for it, so both parents screwed the kid. He must have been about fourteen and was grounded for burning the carpet. His story was that he'd gotten hungry while playing a video game and decided to toast some Pop-Tarts. He couldn't take the time away from the game to toast them properly, so he tried toasting them with a fireplace lighter. When I asked him about it, he replied, "How did I know it would catch the carpet on fire?" I wasn't buying it. He eventually came clean. He was lighting a cigarette, and ashes fell. I asked again. Yes, he was smoking, but it was pot. Did I panic, yell, scream, pray for him, scold him, or talk to him? None of the above. I told him his secret was safe with me. I was a crappy dad, and I was becoming one hell of an enabler.

He was kicked out of school multiple times for his poor behavior. His mother tried to homeschool him for a while, but that didn't work. I can't tell you why. I put my head in the sand and let that be their power struggle. Until his mother had had enough, I believe Paul was sixteen, and she could no longer control him. A good father would have said, "Send him down to me and let me try." But I thought, "If she couldn't make him sociable, how could I?" Bullshit. I was afraid and lazy, and I didn't have the money to raise him, feed him, and clothe him. Again — bullshit. But it made sense in my cowardly, self-centered brain. I didn't want the responsibility and wasn't man enough to own up to it. When it came to taking care of my family, I was my father's son. There were days when I didn't like myself. I blamed his mother. I thought, "She screwed Paul up. Let her deal with it."

I believe in God's plan, and I know everything of consequence happens exactly as it's supposed to, but I wish I'd have fought for my son. His mother decided he was out of control and sent him to a camp for troubled teens in Utah — the Red Mountains, where Butch Cassidy and the Sundance Kid had their Hole in the Wall Gang. It was in the middle of nowhere, so the kids had nowhere to run. I have no proof that the counselors physically abused the kids, but from what Paul has told me, I believe they did, and the few times I visited him, my gut told me something wasn't right. Little did I know about the abusive treatment, including solitary confinement in a closet. I might have known better if I'd cared more, but I didn't want to go against his mom. His stepdad was paying for the camp, and I just went along — like going along with the Nazis without joining the Fascist Party. This abuse, brainwashing, and mind control were all done under the cover of horse training and care as therapy. I love horses, but they are not therapists.

The day he was taken to the camp, two large men wearing hats and weapons physically carried him away. I should have been there. I had the means. I had the time. I chose to bury my head in the sand and let my son be institutionalized. For a time, Paul was better behaved. But before long, the anger returned. He argued constantly with his mom and stepdad. The camp's so-called therapy had tried to solve his problems, but if anything, it made them worse. I continued my pattern of avoidance. I was around, but I wasn't involved.

The Awakening

In his early twenties, Paul's girlfriend gave birth to a beautiful baby boy named Andy. For the first time, I felt something more than ambivalence or a sense of duty toward my son. I was pissed. What an idiot! How could he? I stayed mad at him for more than ten years, until during a huge argument, he asked me a question I couldn't answer. *How could you be mad at me for creating a beautiful baby?*

That moment cracked something open in me. It was a spiritual awakening. I realized that I loved my son and my grandson, no matter when or how he got here. No resentment. No anger. Just unconditional love. And it was perfect. That was a few years ago. Before that, I'd kept my distance — just a call here and there, enough to keep in touch but not really connect. I'd only seen my grandson three times. I didn't like talking to Paul on the phone because he was always angry, and I didn't understand the darkness behind it.

Then, on a business trip to Seattle, I told Paul I could spend the day with him and his girlfriend. We had lunch, saw a movie, and, for the sake of keeping the peace, I took them to a weed shop. Paul had to move his gun from under his seat to the trunk — apparently, you couldn't park at a dispensary with immediate access to a firearm. Why he carries is another story.

I took them to dinner at a fancy steakhouse where I could play the big shot. Of course, I didn't realize that's what I was doing. I thought I was treating my son to a great night when all he wanted was to sit in a park and talk. By dinner, I was drunk. I'd had a few at lunch and snuck drinks during the movie. I picked a fight, told him how stupid he was. How pissed I was. And he asked me that life-altering question. *How could you be mad at me for creating a beautiful baby?* It hit me so hard, I panicked. I felt so much love for him, and so much shame for the way I'd treated him. Instead of sitting with those feelings, I did what I always did — I blew up the conversation with insults, and it spiraled into a shouting match.

"Well, fuck you!" "No, fuck you!"

We parted ways, swearing we were done with each other. I went to the bar — of course I did. Then I saw Paul walking toward me. My drunk, irrational mind panicked. *Was he going to shoot me?* He got closer. Closer. I ducked. But instead of a punch, he wrapped me in a huge bear hug and broke down in tears. "I could never hurt you," he said. "How could you even think that?" I felt relieved. I felt guilty. I told him to go home, that we'd talk. And we did.

For the next few days, we talked for hours. We talked about the horrors of the camp. About how his other parent blamed him for a mental illness he had no control over. I started to understand his anger. And for the first time, I began to accept it. Paul called me out on my selfishness, on the way I compartmentalized everything. And he made one thing very clear: the cycle of shitty dads in our family ended with me. I'd heard him say it before, but never believed it. My ego whispered, *If I couldn't break the cycle, how could he?* I was wrong.

Paul has made life choices that put his son first. He's cut off toxic people to protect Andy. He loves that boy with a devotion I've only seen once before — in my mother. But Paul's love is different. He sets boundaries. When Andy steps out of line, there are consequences. My son is a great dad in spite of me. I gave him a roadmap of what *not* to do, and thank God, he stayed off my path. I still don't communicate enough. But I'm grateful. Grateful that our relationship is stronger than ever. Grateful that I have hope, that I can be more present for my son and grandson. And grateful that my child has finally found the strength to be honest — not just with me, but with the world.

How the Fuck Did I Miss This?

This may explain so much — the anger, the depression that's been there since childhood.

Shortly before I went in for my transplant surgery, Paul kept telling me he had something important to share, but that he was going to wait until I was fully healed. Just knowing there was a revelation waiting on the other side of my surgery was a light in the darkness of my recovery. When the news finally came, it felt like a massive shift—the kind of shift that makes the world a more livable, peaceful place. It was like watching a wild animal finally being set free from a cage.

I'm a lucky man. At sixty-two, I'm going to be there for my child like never before. I love you, my child. I couldn't be happier or prouder of you than I am right now.

And I'm going to have a daughter.

You see, by the time you read this, my son, Paul Henry, will be my daughter, Emily Rose.

EPILOGUE: PROGRESS, NOT PERFECTION

IF THIS WERE A HOLLYWOOD MOVIE, THE SCREEN WOULD fade to black right after that last sentence. The music would swell, the credits would roll, and you would walk away assuming my daughter and I walked off into the sunset together, completely healed.

But this isn't a movie. This is a story about rigorous honesty. And the rigorously honest truth is that things between Emily and me are not great right now.

I love my daughter. I completely accept Emily, and I support transgender folks one hundred percent. But love and acceptance don't magically erase thirty-seven years of baggage, and they don't automatically bridge the massive cultural divide we are standing across.

I am a full-blooded, old-fashioned conservative. Emily knows this, and she is absolutely terrified of the people in my political party. And honestly? I get it. I am embarrassed by my own party's stupid, bigoted position on LGBTQ issues. I see the fear it causes her, and I hate it.

Right now, I keep more distance between us than I would like. But the distance today is very different than the distance I kept when she was growing up. Back then, I stayed away because I was selfish, lazy, and drinking. Today, I keep my distance because I am desperately trying to learn how to relate to her, and I am terrified of doing damage while I figure it out.

I am ignorant. I don't understand the delicate nuances of the conversation required to show 100% support, and because of that, I open my mouth and I say things that hurt her. I stumble over my words, my phrasing is clumsy, and my old-school mentality crashes right into her deeply vulnerable reality.

So, I step back. Not because I don't care, and not because I don't love her, but because I need to learn how to be the father she actually needs.

In A.A., we have a saying: *Progress, not perfection.* I am not the perfect father. I am not even a *good* father yet. But I am sober. I am awake. I am no longer the guy arguing over the exact ingredients of a martini while his life burns down around him. I am a guy looking at his daughter, owning his ignorance, and committing to doing the work, one day at a time.

I don't know exactly what the future holds for Emily and me. But for the first time in my life, I am not running away from it.

I'm just going to keep showing up.